TIME'S ISLAND

TIME'S ISLAND

THE CALIFORNIA DESERT

T.H. WATKINS

PEREGRINE SMITH BOOKS

In association with
The Wilderness Society

The Wilderness society, founded in 1935, is a nonprofit
membership organization devoted to preserving wilderness
and wildlife, protecting America's forests, parks, rivers,
deserts, and shorelands, and fostering an American land
ethic. For further information, write: Membership Services,
The Wilderness Society, 1400 Eye Street NW, Washington,
DC 20005

First edition

92 91 90 89   5 4 3 2 1

This is a Peregrine Smith book, published by Gibbs Smith,
Publisher, P.O. Box 667, Layton, Utah 84041

Design by J. Scott Knudsen

Manufactured in Korea

Library of Congress Cataloging-in-Publication Data
Watkins, T. H. (Tom H.), 1936-
    Time's island : the California desert / [T.H. Watkins].
        p   cm.
    ISBN 0-87905-344-5 (pbk.)
    1. Nature conservation—California—California Desert
National Conservation Area. 2. Natural history—
California—California Desert National Conservation Area.
3. California Desert National Conservation Area
(Calif.)   I. Title.
QH76.5.C2W38   1989   89-8367
508.794—dc20   CIP

This book is for my father—

not only because he is especially

fond of deserts, but because I

am especially fond of him

Contents

Acknowledgments

The author would like to thank all those who took the time to give the manuscript a careful reading, including Norbert Riedy and Patricia Schifferle of The Wilderness Society's California/Nevada regional office in San Francisco, Elden Hughes, director of the California Desert Protection League (who also furnished many of the photographs from the league's collection), and Wallace Stegner.

Prologue

THE DESERT IS BELOW ME, SPREADING OUT TO A GREAT
circle of horizon that is smoky with blue distance. I can see the wide,
U-shaped canyon where I started out 2,500 feet lower and six hours
earlier. I can't see much in the way of vegetation from this height
and distance, but I can remember how startled I was by the abundance I had found there this morning after my father had dropped
me off. It was the most extraordinary mix of desert cacti, grasses,
shrubs, and trees I can remember ever seeing all in one place all at
one time — Mojave yucca and jumping cholla; beavertail and hedge-
hog cacti; creosote bush, greasewood, blackbrush, shadscale, and
saltbrush; Joshua trees, mesquite, desert willow, piñon pine, and juniper.
The scene had possessed the character of a botanical garden painstakingly
landscaped to illustrate the spread of vegetation typical of the eastern Mojave.
I had half expected to see little white signs tacked on to the ends of tiny
spikes jammed into the ground in the shadow of each plant; "Jumping cholla,"
one might have said, *"Opuntia fulgida."*

Now I am surrounded by rock, an abundance of rock. I am, in fact,
sitting on rock, a huge slab that is balanced at the lip of a steep ravine choked
with more rock, boulders the size of small Japanese automobiles piled one
on top of the other like a long stony cascade that has finally come to rest.
In the interstices of these jumbled stones beavertail cactus, tough, twisted
little piñon pines, and spiky yucca plants have somehow made a home. In
the little flat at the foot of the ravine are more stones. Others pile around
the foot and fill the clefts of a ridge lower than the one on which I sit. On
the other side of that ridge are still more stones, and beyond that another
rocky flat and another stony ridge, then another, and another, in a kind of
gigantic cluttered stairway that leads down to the gentle valley through which
an old ranch road snakes its way like a dusty whip.

Behind and above me is more rock, a precipitous stone wall rising maybe
three hundred feet. This has stopped me, but not until I have dragged my
middle-aged heft over all the ridges below and have scrambled a hundred
yards up the incline of the dark and crowded ravine at the head of which
I now sit. The stones in that narrow slit were so steeply balanced that for
all their size I could not help but fear that one false move would send a couple of million pounds of them down on me, leaving my crushed and desic-
cated corpse buried under so much rock that it would remain undiscovered
during this and all subsequent geological periods. It had been at the most

The boulder-strewn landscape of the New York Mountains, East Mojave National Scenic Area. (T. H. Watkins)

nerve-wracking moment of that climb, when I had one toe jammed into a miniscule crack and my fingernails imbedded in another, my glance fixed on the unstable pile of geology stacked high above me, that a jet from (I supposed) George Air Force Base had chosen to break the sound barrier somewhere in the limitless sky, sending the unbelievable thunderclap of a violent sonic boom echoing through the shattered mountains. I am a dead person, I had told myself.

But the rocks had not moved, and so here I sit, breathless but safe. I open my bottle of water and my bag of gorp for lunch. A thin spray of clouds is fanned out like chalk dust across the dark blue sky above the edge of the sand-colored rock wall looming over me. I had hoped to get over that edge and stand at the summit to see what was on the other side, but I know now that I will never be able to climb that chunk of stone. No matter. There is plenty of desert to see from where I am.

Where I am is the New York Mountains, an enormous garden of stone in the East Mojave National Scenic Area, California. I am perhaps four hard hours of driving from the shrieking caldron of downtown Los Angeles, and the quiet that envelopes me here is complete and satisfying. This is what I came here for—to spend some time alone in the desert to get a feeling for what it has to offer in the way of sanctuary and beauty, to provide the weight of observed reality to the words I will be using to describe this country and what has happened to it and what should happen to it and what is likely to happen to it if we do not seize the opportunity to save it.

But the trip also is a kind of homecoming. This is my country, as I am fond of telling my desert-deprived colleagues in the effete and humid East; I was born and reared in the San Bernardino Valley seventy miles east of Los Angeles—a valley that was itself the living exemplar of a high-desert landscape only a little diminished by what humans had done to it since the first colonizing Mormons had settled the place in the early 1850s. Even San Bernardino, the region's largest community, surrounded on all sides by groves of orange trees and backwalled on the north by the long blue line of the San Bernardino Mountains, had possessed the dusty look of a desert town during most of the years in which I had known it, living out the dictum of historian Walter Prescott Webb that most of the West is "semi-desert with a desert heart." Now redevelopment had transmogrified the central part of town and urbanization had spread out from the city to obliterate the orange groves and almost all of the valley's natural character, covering it with an ooze of concrete, asphalt, fast-food strips, condominium clusters, and lawns and golf courses the color and consistency of pool-table tops.

The story of what has happened to the San Bernardino Valley, I think as I sit upon my rock, is a kind of cautionary tale to which the stewards of what is left of the original California Desert might pay attention. It is the story of how circumstance can alter the character of a place and make it less than what it was—and can do it so quickly that a generation is enough to witness the change. My father, who has been driving us around the country in his sturdy old Ford pickup over the past several days, has spent most of his life in and around this desert. "I'll never live long enough to see it all," he has told me at one point during our journeying, and he clearly regrets that fact. Still, he has seen more of the desert than anybody I know and loves it better than most. He remembers it from the depression days, when the Federal Music Project of the Works Progress Administration—the New Deal's famous WPA—funded his small western band as it played its way around the hamlets of the Mojave on the little vaudeville circuit, and for nearly thirty years after the war he and my mother launched frequent sorties into the desert to see what they could see, taking the six children with them in the early years, then wandering the country on their own when the children were grown. She is gone now, and so is much of the desert he remembers, and I have watched him from time to time shake his head silently, pipe gripped in his mouth, saying nothing and not needing to, as he looked out over one more housing development, one more shopping center, one more gas station that stood on land that he had known once as a wild and empty place.

But there is still desert for the saving. In just the past four days, over maybe eight hundred miles of driving, we have seen an incredible sweep of country, much of it still wild and deserving to stay wild—the pine forests of the Inyo Mountains along the southernmost wall of the Sierra Nevada, the white sands of the Eureka Dunes glimmering under a dull morning sun north of Death Valley, the jagged redrock walls of Hanging Rock Canyon in the Last Chance Range, the Panamint Range lifting over Death Valley like a great breaking wave, the flat, white shining expanse of Silver Dry Lake between the Soda Mountains and the Hollow Hills. We have seen places whose names ring with the incomparable music of poetry, hope, and irony that its settlers and passersby have laid on the land—the El Paso Mountains and the Saddle Peak Hills, Chimney Peak and the Golden Valley, Joshua Flats and the Last Chance Range, the Ibex Hills and Cima Dome, Rainbow Wells and the Kingston Mountains, the Nopah Range and the Funeral Mountains, a couple of dozen more mountains and hills and valleys and canyons and dunes and springs and dry lakes under a forgiving November sun, and I know we will see dozens more in the days and miles to come.

Some of this country I know well myself, some of it I do not, and some of it I am seeing for the first time; but all of it has resonance for me, a powerful bringing forth of half-remembered moments: waking by the side of the spring-full Mojave River, hearing the unfamiliar chuckle of water over stones and marveling at the fact that a celebration of flowers has miraculously been rolled out on the desert floor like a carpet, flowers I have never seen before and will never see again; walking with my Boy Scout troop somewhere in the Little San Bernardino Mountains and coming across the enormous dry husk of a long-dead horse, a death so clean that it robs the event of mystery; climbing the endless sliding hill of a sand dune—in the Kelso Dunes?—at around the age of five, trying to fight my way to the top, my tiny legs finally giving it up; learning the sensory properties of heat: the dry, ponderous weight of heat on the body under a dangerous noon sun, the wavery look of things through the rising heat reflected from the ground, the scorching pain of slick, flat rocks as hot as stovetops; climbing up a pile of dusty red rocks and sand to the curving edge of the crater at the top of an ancient cinder cone, slowly turning to marvel that I can view the full circle of the horizon; starting landslides down the side of another old mountain with a gaggle of raucous teenaged companions, all of us watching and laughing with the mindless glee of natural vandals as boulders career a thousand feet to the valley floor; holding my breath for what seems like a century as I spy on an old coyote drifting like smoke through scattered clumps of creosote bush; seeing for the first time a Joshua tree forest, a palm tree oasis, a cinder cone, a sunset, a hard, white moon floating in a universe of stars. . . .

And so I sit on my rock in the New York Mountains, looking out over forty miles of outdoors, wondering if the memories will give what I need to say about this place, this desert that speaks to me out of the past and the present, enough strength to make it real. While I consider this, a golden eagle slides up a spiral of air from the valley floor, then curves over the lip of the stone wall above me and disappears on the other side, going easily where muscle and desire have failed to carry me.

THE PLACE
1. North to Amargosa

THE 25.5 MILLION ACRES—OR MORE than 39,000 square miles—that spill down the map in a rough 320-mile fan from the southernmost extension of the Sierra Nevada to the Mexican border encompass what is generally called the California Desert. The term is a misnomer, as such things often are, for the area in fact takes in not one but at least two desert systems, and very likely three: the Sonoran Desert spreading up into the valley of the Colorado River from southern Arizona, northern Mexico, and Baja California; the Great Basin Desert creeping in from southern Nevada; and the Mojave Desert, which occupies the heart of the region between Death Valley National Monument on the north, Joshua Tree National Monument on the south, the juncture of the Tehachapis with the San Gabriel Mountains on the west, and the Colorado River on the east. Some plant biologists argue that the Mojave itself is not a distinct system, but an enormous transition zone between the Great Basin Desert and the Sonoran Desert (which, as an added confusion, usually is identified as the Colorado Desert for that portion of it which resides in California).

However it is identified and divided, the California Desert is an indisputably enormous region united by the same fact that unites most of that part of the American West lying between the Rocky Mountains and the Sierra Nevada and the Canadian and Mexican borders: aridity. Here, aridity is not merely a condition, it is a force to be reckoned with. It has determined the character of the landscape, the kind of plant and animal life contained within it, and the course of such human events as have been connected with it, and it defines the country more precisely than any human boundaries could hope to do. Which is not to say that it is a uniform thing, however unifying. Overall, the California Desert receives 11 inches or less of rain per year, but in any given spot or in any given year that amount can vary considerably. In Big Pine, at the northern extremity of the desert region, for example, an average of nearly 11 inches of rain does in fact fall yearly, while less than a hundred miles to the southeast, the floor of Death Valley averages only 1.7 inches—and some years in Death Valley there is no rain at all for a full twelve months or longer. All of which helps to explain why only two rivers worthy of the designation (and there is some question about that) originate in the California Desert—the Mojave coming out of the San Bernardino Mountains in the south and the Amargosa coming out of the Spring Mountains of Nevada in the north—and why even these are inclined to disappear altogether during years when precipitation falls below the average.

Ironically, while there is precious little water to be felt or seen in the desert, there is the memory of plenty of it: scores of big and little dry lakes, or playas—remnants of ancient seas that once covered huge territories—are scattered from Roach Dry Lake in southern Nevada to Ford Dry Lake in Southern California, more than three hundred miles away. The present Salton Sea—the largest body of water in the whole region—was the site of one such remnant, though its present lake level is the result of floods on the Colorado River from 1905 through 1907 and subsequent irrigation runoff, not the residue of geological waters.

Rainstorm in the Kelso Dunes, East Mojave.
(Terrence Moore)

Salt flat on the floor of
Death Valley. (Suzi
Moore)

Upper Warm Spring in the Saline Valley, one of the few natural springs in the California Desert. (Jim Dodson/California Desert Protection League)

The memory of violence, too, is another unifying factor in the California Desert, as it is for most of the continent between the Rocky Mountains and the Pacific Coast. For this is the place where great collisions and uplifts and fracturing took place over the course of hundreds of millions of years, as continental plates and the pieces of continental plates slammed into one another, ground against one other, and slid underneath or over one another, the whole slow-moving but nonetheless catastrophic business shoving mountain ranges into the sky, wrinkling the skin of the earth, rending and shattering its deepest rocks, giving birth to the sputter and fire of volcanoes that rose like buboes on the cracked and trembling surface, spilling glowing rivers of lava across the stony land. From the abrupt eastern escarpment of the Sierra Nevada to Amboy Crater in the center of the Mojave Desert, the protocols of geological time can still be read in the California Desert. And felt—for this deeply fractured and unstable land is the home of earthquakes that periodically broadcast waves of

movement through the country like the echoes of past cataclysms.

There is a final unifying matter to be considered. All but about 7 million acres of the California Desert is in federal ownership (the 7 million are owned by the state or are in private ownership). Some 3 million acres of this are taken up by enormous military installations like the Naval Weapons Center/Fort Irwin complex north of Barstow and the Marine Corps Air Ground Combat Center north of Twentynine Palms. The rest is public land—part of the American public lands system. A little over 2 million acres of this are included in Death Valley National Monument, and a little under 550,000 in Joshua Tree National Monument, both administered by the National Park Service of the Department of the Interior. The remaining 12.1 million acres are under the administration of the Bureau of Land Management, another Interior Department agency. All of these nearly 15 million acres of public land administered by these public agencies are the shared inheritance of every citizen of the United States and by law they are to be managed in the best interests of both the land and the public. It is a thought worth keeping in mind.

If aridity, remembered violence, and public ownership provide the various desert regions with a common bond, geological variations and disparities in rainfall have conspired with the mix of desert systems to give the landscape a complexity that defies its frequent description as little more than a collection of subtleties. True, there are no Grand Canyons and no Grand Tetons here, and for those who demand that level of operatic drama in their geomorphology, the desert is likely to be a disappointment. But the place has its own kind of drama, for those who are willing to consider something more than picture-postcard scenery, and the rewards that can come from getting off the big state and interstate highways and stopping to take a look around are such that they can pull the viewer back again and again until his regard and his heart have been captured permanently.

Consider, for example, the roughly 8,000 square miles of desert contained in a wide belt running between Cajon Pass, the long notch in the San Bernardino Mountains that connects San Bernardino and Victorville, and Owens Lake, a huge dry lake in the shadow of the Sierra Nevada (unlike the remnant playas that punctuate the desert, Owens Lake is dry because of the human diversion of water from the Owens River, about which more later). Just twenty-five miles north of Edwards Air Force Base — where NASA's space shuttles most often touch down — lies a place called the Golden Valley, a gently rolling vale between the Almond Mountains and the Lava Mountains where, during wet years, the springtime display of brittlebrush and four-o'clocks, purple mat and sand verbena, pale trumpets and Mojave aster, lupine, desert bell, horseweed, desert chicory, and many other species of desert wildflowers can spread explosions of color that transform this desert place with its backdrop of amber-colored mountains into an impressionist's garden — at least for a time. A little over twenty miles to the northwest lies an area few people would ever mistake for a garden, but one that could be mistaken for a piece of the canyon country of southern Utah: the sandy badlands and narrow redrock canyons of the El Paso Mountains,

Barrel cactus in the Kingston Mountains, East Mojave. (Terrence Moore)

Upthrust and fractured stone in the Soda Mountains. (Elden Hughes/California Desert Protection League)

The lower Saline Valley, where seeps and springs and occasional rains turn the grasses lush. (Mike McWherter/California Desert Protection League)

A flowering yucca in the rolling hills of the Golden Valley. (Rose Certini/California Desert Protection League)

Bristlecone pines are among the oldest forms of life on the planet. This one is seen in the White Mountains on the northern edge of the California Desert. (Terrence Moore)

A view of the snow-draped eastern escarpment of the Sierra Nevada from the White Mountains north of Death Valley. (Mike McWherter/California Desert Protection League)

a wall of upthrust and fractured stone along the line of the Garlock Fault that is dominated by a 5,244-foot extinct volcano called Black Mountain. Less than twenty miles north of the El Paso Mountains begins another, infinitely more impressive, mountain wall—the long, gray eastern escarpment of the Sierra Nevada, which rises shark-toothed and magnificent above the floor of the Owens River Valley. The major peaks of this sweep of mountains—Mt. Jenkins, Owens Peak, Lamont Peak, Sawtooth Peak, and Chimney Peak—are all at or very near 8,000 feet and, with piney forests cloaking their shoulders, bear comparison to such alpine silhouettes as the High Uintas of Utah or the Minarets of the central Sierra Nevada; yet to reach them from the east you will climb steeply through successive bands of desert vegetation, through fields of the ubiquitous creosote bush, patches of cholla and yucca and beavertail cactus, orchards of stunted Joshua trees, groves of juniper and piñon pine. From the floor of the valley to the spine of the Sierra Nevada, this is high desert as high and as wild as you can find it anywhere on the continent.

Climb high enough into these mountains—to 7,000 thousand feet, say—and on a clear day you could see, if not forever, at least sixty miles east by northeast across the China Lake Naval Weapons Center and the Argus Range to the Panamint Range on the western edge of Death Valley, a mountain complex whose own moon-raking crags—dominated by the 11,049-foot Telescope Peak—are more than a match for those in which you stand. And within your line of sight—theoretically, at least—would be a stretch of territory that contains astonishing variety across just ninety degrees of the horizon. Looking clockwise and beginning at about nine o'clock, you would have within the hypothetical compass of your vision the Coso Range some forty miles north, an area of volcanic tablelands whose glistening outcrops of pure obsidian have provided weapons, tools, and ornaments since prehistoric times and whose geothermal springs send whispers of steam into the desert air. At ten o'clock would be Darwin Falls, a small, green splendor of ferns and reeds and mosses, streams, pools, and waterfalls—a tiny Eden tucked into the stony canyons of the northern end of the Argus Range. Just over ten miles to the north of Darwin Falls, if you could bend your line of sight over the Santa Rosa Hills and into Mill Canyon, you would see the rare "star dunes," an oddly shaped complex of sand dunes that have been swept up and shaped by the winds that curl against the slopes at the northern end of the canyon. Finally, turning your glance to somewhere between eleven o'clock and noon, you would take in the unique hanging—or "goblet"—valleys of the central Panamint Range, a series of bowl-shaped little mountain valleys that overhang the long Panamint Valley on the western side of the range. Well-watered (by desert standards) with runoff from the mountain peaks above them, these small, beautiful valleys support a richly various plant community, from creosote bush and cacti at the lower elevations to desert willow, cottonwoods, and cattails along the streams that course through the valleys, as well as generous stands of juniper and piñon pine at the higher elevations. In spots they bear a powerful family resemblance to some of the high mountain valleys of the Rockies, yet they sit hugging the western slopes of a mountain range that forms the western rim of an area that is almost universally perceived as the definitive American desert: Death Valley.

A yucca in full bloom in Grass Valley. (Elden Hughes/California Desert Protection League)

THERE IS NOTHING SUBTLE ABOUT Death Valley, nor is there anything in it reminiscent of sylvan glades or the classical landscapes of, say, the Turnerian school. It is harsh, brutally real, and unforgivingly beautiful, a place where life in all its forms is pared to the core. This may have been the earth in its beginnings, and standing on the floor of the valley it is not difficult to imagine those epochs when fire and steam filled the air and mountains rose and fell. Or perhaps this is what the earth will be in its ending, as John C. Van Dyke speculated nearly a century ago: "Is then this great expanse of sand and rock the beginning of the end? Is that the way our globe shall perish? Who can say? Nature plans the life, she plans the death; it must be that she plans aright."

Death Valley itself is indeed a great expanse. At a little more than two million acres, it represents a shade over 8 percent of the entire 25.5 million acres of the California Desert. If one includes the 563,540 acres in the neighboring Eureka and Saline valleys and the Last Chance

Close-up of a blossoming desert candle at Blackwater Well. (Elden Hughes/California Desert Protection League)

The hidden splendor
called Darwin Falls.
(Suzi Moore)

Range north of the official boundary of the monument (as many would have us do), the figure exceeds 10 percent—more than 4,000 square miles of desert, a territory twice the size of the state of Delaware and lightyears beyond it or any other state in the experience of elemental life it offers.

Begin with the Saline Valley just off the northwest quadrant of Death Valley's national monument territory. It is a long valley bounded on the east by the jumbled foothills of the Cottonwood Mountains and on the west by the upthrust eastern edge of the Inyo Mountains, an abrupt mountain wall jammed into the sky with a drama that rivals that of the Sierra Nevada looming over the Owens River Valley farther west. Its looming triangular peaks, often snow-girt in the fall and winter, provide a spectacular backdrop for the Saline Dunes piled against the foothills of the mountains, one of the most beautiful and least-known dune systems in the country. Much the same could be said of most of the rest of the region from the Nelson Range in the south to the Saline Range in the north (which butts against Joshua Flats in the Cowhorn Valley, where the northernmost stand of Joshua trees spread their arms). It is country hard to get to and consequently offers one of the increasingly rare (even in the desert) opportunities for absolute solitude; the Saline Range is so little visited, in fact, that its highest peak was not climbed until 1973.

Over the crest of the Saline Range lies the broad Eureka Valley, with the peaks of the Last Chance Range curving south by southwest to bracket it on the east. At the southern foot of this valley is another dune system, one considerably better known and more often visited than the Saline Dunes twenty-five miles to the southwest. These are the Eureka Dunes, designated a national natural landmark in 1983, and with good reason: with a curtain made up of multicolored bands of stratified rock in the Last Chance Range behind them and with one dune that rises 700 feet—making this sand "mountain" the highest west of Great Sand Dunes National Monument in Colorado—the nine square miles of this system may be the most visually impressive of any in the desert. North of the dunes is Hanging Rock Canyon, a ragged redrock slit in the Last Chance Range that connects the wide Eureka Valley with the narrower, shallower trough of land called North Death Valley, the northernmost extension of Death Valley itself.

Cattails in Darwin Spring. (Terrence Moore)

Past Ubehebe Crater just inside the northern boundary of the national monument, the tonguelike valley begins to spread out the farther south—and farther down—one travels, sinking below sea level for the first time at a point just about 6 miles above Mud Canyon, then going deeper into the crust of the earth with each passing mile until the lowest spot on the North American continent—282 feet below sea level—is reached just above the undrinkable spring called Badwater. It is the valley floor, 120 miles long and less than 10 wide for most of its length, that has given this place its stygian reputation, with its summertime temperatures whose highs aver-

A tiny cataract in
Hunter Canyon of the
Inyo Mountains.
(Terrence Moore)

Windrows on a slope of
the Eureka Dunes,
Eureka Valley. (Terrence
Moore)

A salt flat under the
Greenwater Mountains
on the southeastern
border of Death Valley.
(Mike
McWherter/California
Desert Protection
League)

age 116 degrees in July (but once hit a record of 134 degrees), its nearly waterless environment, its 14 square miles of sand dunes, its tiny patches of saltgrass and pickleweed, and its 200 square miles of shimmering, crystalline salt flats — some of the debris left behind when the Pleistocene body of water called Lake Manley receded during the final centuries of the last ice age 14,000 or 15,000 years ago.

It may be the valley floor that gives Death Valley its reputation as a hard place to find a living, but it is the mountains that rise above it on all sides that give it character and a painterly beauty matched nowhere else in the California Desert. Telescope Peak in the Panamint Range tops out at more than 11,000 feet, and while the peaks in the Funeral Mountains and Black Mountains on the eastern side of the valley are less toplofty, six of them climb to perfectly respectable heights ranging from 5,033 feet to 6,703

feet — altitudes made all the more impressive by the fact that the mountains are usually seen from a vantage point considerably below sea level. The slopes and peaks of the mountains are made equally remarkable by the fact that they are a kaleidescope of pastels whose tone and color shift with the passage of the sun across the sky and the seasons across the year — misty reds and pinks and blues and purples move like shadows over the distant mountainscape, giving it the character of some mythic kingdom hovering at the edge of imagination. Georgia O'Keeffe would have loved to paint this place.

THERE IS INDISPUTABLE VARIETY then, and beauty to spare, to be found in just the ragged triangle of desert from Cajon Pass to Big Pine, the Eureka Valley to the southern foot of Death Valley, where the Amargosa River trickles down from Nevada and around the Ibex Hills to disappear into the sand beneath the Owlshead Mountains. Beauty and variety, but, one has to admit, not much that invites human settlement and the cultivation of civilization and the domestic arts. This is certainly true of Death Valley, that hardest of all desert places, and it is no less true of most of the rest of the California Desert. Yet even in the heart of the most inhospitable valleys and the twisting, arid canyons of the most distant mountains, humanity has invested its interest and left its mark. We are a stubborn species, tougher than we know, and for millennia we have been making a habit of trying to live where the land does not welcome us.

THE PEOPLE

THE ROCK WALLS AND LARGER boulders in at least three of the many narrow canyons sliced into the basaltic stone of the Coso Range west of Death Valley are richly ornamented with thousands of pictographs and petroglyphs — the splendid graffiti of an age that precedes any other kind of human record. (Pictographs are paintings done with colors obtained from hematite, limonite, kaolinite, manganese and other naturally occurring minerals; petroglyphs are drawings that have been incised in the rock by removing the blue-black oxides on its surface — called "desert varnish" — either by scraping through it or by "pecking" at it with another, harder stone.) The Coso Range is one of the most abundant sites of such primordial etchings, but it is by no means the only one. Inscription Canyon in the mountains above Rainbow Basin National Natural Landmark north of Barstow contains a similar number of drawings, and thousands more are scattered throughout the entire California Desert region, from the southernmost end of the Colorado River Valley to the northwest quadrant of the Mojave Desert.

Some of the drawings have been around long enough to have been obscured by another coat of desert varnish; some of these have been carbon-dated back to 9000 B.C., not too many centuries after rising ocean waters cut off the Bering "land bridge" between Siberia and Alaska, across which the original peoples of the American continents had come. Others are so fresh-looking they might have been scratched out in our own time, though they more likely date from sometime in the nineteenth century.

The drawings, then, provide a unique record of human participation in the life of the California Desert over the course of at least ninety centuries, from the time when the climate was still temperate enough in some areas to support forestland and swamps and the abundant wildlife contained within them, to the age of the archaeologist. Rich in the kind of symbolism that would drive a Jungian psychologist to frenzies of speculation, as well as the more immediately comprehensible stylized renderings of animals and human beings, the drawings doubtless would have extraordinary tales to tell, if only we could decipher them with any certainty. We do make an educated guess that most of them were done to commemorate or accompany the ceremonials attached to such occasions as the attainment of puberty, the act of mating, giving birth, appeasing and propitiating the gods, or dying. Others almost certainly were drawn to mark great events in the life of a tribe or band or individual family — abundant harvests, successful hunts, brave exploits against cowardly enemies, that sort of thing — and still others probably conveyed such mundane information as directions to water sources, campsites, and hunting grounds. And some may have been no more (and no less) than expressions of the artistic impulse, as those who occupied that percentage of genius common to all human populations — the kinds of people whose psychic energy, intellectual curiosity, and creative drive probably gave birth to the remarkable complexities of language and mythology expressed in most primitive cultures — turned their instincts and their talents loose on the primeval stone.

By the sixteenth century, most of the artists and record keepers had vanished with the cultures that had produced them, and the native people

Petroglyphs incised through desert varnish on a boulder in Chuckwalla Mountains. (Terrence Moore)

of the California Desert had dwindled down to a precious few individual tribes with a total population that probably did not much exceed ten thousand people—who got a fair living off the inhospitable land probably because there *were* so few of them. Some of the groups were so small that tribe may be too capacious a term to describe them; the Koso Indians, also called the Panamints, for example, may have had no more than 150 members scattered through the Coso, Argus, Panamint, and Funeral ranges around Death Valley.

For all the size of any single band, however, native populations were well represented throughout most of the desert region. More than 130 miles to the southwest of the Koso territory, all through the southeastern slope of the Tehachapi Mountains, lived the tribelet called the Kawausu, while in the northern foothills of the San Bernardino Mountains the more numerous (perhaps 1,500) and nomadic Serrano held sway, ranging through much of the Mojave Desert as far west as the San Gabriel Mountains and as far northeast as the territory of another people called the Chemehuevi, about 1,000 of whom occupied

(or at least roamed through) a long band of territory that extended south of Death Valley through the Kingston Range, the Providence Mountains, the Coxcomb Mountains, and possibly even the Chuckwalla Mountains north of the Imperial Valley. If so, their territory would have been not far removed from that of the Cahuilla, a comparatively sedentary group of perhaps 2,500 who inhabited the San Bernardino Valley, San Gorgonio Pass (including the area that would become Palm Springs), and the Coachella Valley above the northern end of the Salton Sink (which, after much of it filled with water again at the turn of this century, became the Salton Sea). Directly east, beyond the territory of the Cahuilla and the Chemehuevi, lay the Yuma Indians at the southern end of the Colorado River Valley, and north of them lived a band called the Halchidoma, who acted as a kind of buffer tribe between the Yuma and the most populous and vigorous of all the California Desert's native people—the Mojave.

The name (variously spelled *Mohave*) is a corruption of that which they had for themselves—*Aha macave,* meaning "the people who live along the water." The name was admirably precise, for the roughly four thousand Mojave people who were represented in twenty-two totemic clans occupied the floodplain on both sides of the Colorado River from a point just below the site of today's Hoover Dam to about one hundred miles south of the site of Parker Dam. With the exception of the hunting and trapping of desert cottontails and black-tailed jackrabbits—both of which furnished most of the meat, skins, and fur utilized by these Indians—and forays into the mountain ranges west of the river valley for desert bighorn and other game, the Mojave were an agricultural people who depended upon the annual flooding of the river for the cultivation of corn, squash, and beans. Their dependence upon the river was colorfully expressed in the creation myth that outlined the work of Mastamho, son of the great god Matavilya. The story was charmingly retold by A. L. Kroeber, himself the Great Ancestor of cultural anthropology:

> *In four steps Mastamho strode far north, plunged his cane of breath and spittle into the earth, and the river flowed out. Entering a boat, Mastamho journeyed with mankind to the sea, twisting and tilting the boat or letting it run straight as he wished wide bottom lands or sharp canyons to frame the river. He returned with the people in his arms, surmounted the rising waters to the Mountain Akokahumi, trod the waters down, and took his followers upstream to the northern end of what was to be the Mohave country. Here he heaped up the great pointed peak Avikwame . . . Newberry or Dead Mountain as the Americans call it, where he . . . built himself a house. It is of this house that shamans dream, for here their shadows were as little boys in the face of Mastamho, and received from him their sacred powers. . . . Here, too, Mastamho made the people shout, and the fourth time day and sun and moon appeared. . . .*
>
> *Now Mastamho's work was nearly done. [He taught the Mojave] to farm, to cook in pottery, to speak and count as was best fit for them, and to stay in the country. Then, meditating as to his own end, he stretched his arms, grew into . . . the fish eagle, and flew off, without power or recollection, ignorant and infested with vermin.*

As a result of this uncommonly specific attachment to a single place, Kroeber went on to explain, the Mojave "think in terms of themselves

as a national entity. . . . They think also of their land as a country. . . . With such proclivities, it is small wonder that the petty Californian feuds of locality and inherited revenge have given way among the Mohave to a military spirit, under which the tribe acted as a unit in offensive and defensive enterprise." For neither the Mojave nor any other of the desert tribes, of course, would offensive and defensive enterprise be enough to stay the inevitable when the Stone Age met the Iron Age in this arid new-world landscape.

During a military expedition for roads in 1863, Captain John Ross paused for a portrait with Mojave chief Tercherrum somewhere near the Colorado River. (Courtesy of the Bancroft Library, University of California, Berkeley)

I N OCTOBER 1540, THE COMMANDER of the first band of Europeans to set foot in the California Desert—or anywhere else in California, for that matter—met an ignominious and very painful end. His name was Captain Melchior Diaz. He was the leader of the force of cavalry that had been attached to the great exploring expedition of Francisco Vasquez de Coronado, sent out in February from San Miguel de Culiacan, a primitive garrison town that sat like a scab on the plain of Mexico's northwest littoral beneath the sawtooth wilderness of the

Pictographs on a rock southwest of Joshua Tree National Monument. (Suzi Moore)

A startlingly realistic depiction of a desert bighorn sheep near the site of Fort Piute in the Piute Range above the Colorado River. (Elden Hughes/California Desert Protection League)

Sierra Madre Occidental. The expedition was after gold and other treasures that, it was said, would be found in the mysterious lands to the north of Mexico. After reaching the desert country of southern Arizona (and finding nothing but the treasureless adobe towns of the Zuni Indians), Coronado had sent Diaz and his troop of cavalry west to rendezvous with the seagoing leg of the expedition at the Colorado River.

Sometime in October Diaz and his men had reached the river and learned from local Indians that the expedition's ships had come and gone at least a month earlier. Since they already had come this far, the explorers decided to cross the river on brush rafts and see what there was to see on the other side in a land that already was called California but into which no European had yet ventured. (California would not be officially discovered until 1542, when João Rodriguez Cabrilho, a Portuguese explorer in the employ of Spain, anchored in San Diego Bay.) After getting safely to the other side with their horses, the men headed west in the general direction of the Salton Sink. Along the way, they hunted rabbits for food, chasing after the swift, leather-tough little desert creatures on their horses, spearing them at full gallop with their lances. This was a chancy business, and on one such rabbit hunt somewhere between the Algodones Dunes and the Chocolate Mountains, Captain Diaz miscalculated and became the first European to die on California soil; at full tilt, the blade of his lance sliced into the ground and its butt caught him in the belly, impaling him.

Diaz's men buried him and returned east to hook up again with the Coronado expedition, which wandered clear up into Kansas before the luckless and exhausted conquistadors straggled back to Mexico in 1542. For most of the next three centuries, the California Desert would remain pretty much a blank in the minds of the European settlers of the continent. Father Francisco Eusebio Kino may have explored some of its southern reaches in 1701, but it was not until 1769 that a land expedition from Baja passed through the desert on its way to colonize San Diego, and not until 1776 that a reliable route across the desert between northwest Mexico and the Spanish settlements of California was established—and an uprising of Yuma Indians in 1781 effectively closed this until well into the nineteenth century. (Such uprisings were rare, even among the intermittently aggressive Yuma and Mojave Indians, and by the early nineteenth

century disease and depredations of one kind or another at the hands of the Spanish-Mexican settlers of California had severely reduced an already diminished native population; the American settlers and conquerors soon to come would pretty much finish the job.)

The desert remained a place across which non-Indians passed on their way to somewhere else for at least another generation. The first Americans to do so probably were members of a troop of mountain men and fur-trapping entrepreneurs who were led into Southern California via the Mojave Desert and Cajon Pass by Jedediah Smith in 1826. Smith and his men did not stay long, being ordered out of the territory by the suspicious Mexican Governor, José Maria Echeandia, who feared that they were actually a band of *Yanqui* spies. General Stephen Watts Kearny led his Army of the West across the southern desert to San Diego during the Mexican War of 1846–1848, and during that same war the Mormon Battalion marched across the Mojave Desert to San Bernardino. A great many more came a few years later during the gold rush. In the peak years of 1849 and 1850, an estimated 10,000 gold seekers entered California via the well-named *jornado del muerto* through the glaring desert of southern Arizona, crossing the Colorado River at its confluence with the Gila then staggering west through the long, shallow valleys of the southern stretch of California Desert until they reached the puny settlements at San Bernardino, Los Angeles, or San Diego.

Fruitless dreaming: an abandoned Mexican *arastra* (ore-grinding site) in the Marl Mountains. (Elden Hughes/California Desert Protection League)

Valley!" then faced away. . . . Many accounts have been given to the world as to the origin of the name and by whom it was thus designated but ours were the first visible footsteps, and we the party which named it the saddest and most dreadful name that came to us first from its memories.

No other gold-rush emigrants ever tried the Death Valley route once word of what had happened to Manly and his companions became generally known, but the great infection called the gold rush would permanently affect the California Desert—as it did much of the West—by investing it with the hope that somewhere in this new country, with its limitless horizons, stark mountain ranges, and narrow canyons so often ornamented with the tantalizing scrawls of ancient peoples (secret codes showing the way to hidden treasures?), there must be immeasurable wealth in gold and silver just lying there ready to be snatched up by anyone with the gumption to go after it. It was a reputation as little deserved as it was impossible to eradicate; it is, in fact, with us still. Mary Austin, who knew the desert as well as anyone who ever wrote about it, saw this peculiar obsession as the product of a conspiracy between hope and the mythic wonder of the place itself: "The palpable sense of mystery in the desert air breeds fables, chiefly of lost treasure," she wrote in *the Land of Little Rain* in 1903. "Somewhere within its stark borders, if one believes report, is a hill strewn with nuggets; one seamed with virgin silver; an old clayey water-bed where Indians scooped up earth to make cooking pots and shaped them reeking with grains of pure gold."

If such fables were not enough to sustain the obsession, there *was* gold and silver to be found here and there in the desert—never in quantities that justified the dimensions of all the dreaming after it, but enough to keep that dreaming virulent for generations. One of the first energizing fables was that of something called the Lost Gunsight Mine, which reputedly had been discovered, then its location lost, by a member of the Manly party of 1849. In 1860, the search for this legend led Dr. Dennis French and a few companions into the Argus and Coso ranges, where some minor gold deposits were, in fact, found. Over the years, similarly small discoveries were made in the Slate and Panamint ranges and in the El Paso Mountains. In 1865, rich, though not very large, deposits of galena—silver in combination with lead—were found at a place called

As late as 1915, little hardscrabble mining enterprises in the Ibex Hills above Death Valley were still being supplied by "jackass express"—and the feral descendants of many of these animals still plod around in the mountains of the desert. (Courtesy of the Bancroft Library, University of California, Berkeley)

But there was at least one group of forty-niners which tried it another way. This was a wagon train of about one hundred people who, in December 1849, did not want to wait until the following spring thaw had cleared the passes over the central Sierra Nevada. They decided to attempt a southern route out of Salt Lake City that would lead them southwesterly across the Great Basin and into a long, empty, bitterly arid wilderness just over the Grapevine Mountains at the Nevada border, a place that some called the Valley of Burning Silence—though it would soon enough be given the name by which we know it today. Most of the wagons got into this nearly waterless valley in fair shape, but there was neither water nor grass enough on the valley floor to support the train's oxen, much less its people—and there was no way out that would accommodate wagons. At least fourteen people died on the journey, and it took nearly two months for all the survivors to escape the valley. One of them, William Lewis Manly—whose name is commemorated in Manly Peak in the southern Panamint Range—remembered their last sight of the place. "Just as we were ready to leave," he wrote in his memoirs,

we took off our hats, and then overlooking the scene of so much trial, suffering and death spoke the thought uppermost saying:—"Good bye Death

Two pairs short of the classic twenty-mule affair, this borax team hauls ore out of the mountains above Death Valley sometime around the turn of the century. (Courtesy of the Bancroft Library, University of California, Berkeley)

Water, like food and everything else, had to be hauled in to the borax mines. The team here is carrying out ore and an empty water tank, probably through Towne Pass west of Death Valley. (Courtesy of the Bancroft Library, University of California, Berkeley)

Faster than the standard mule team, though not nearly as maneuverable, a number of steam tractors were used in the borax trade right up to the time of World War I. (Courtesy of the Bancroft Library, University of California, Berkeley)

Cerro Gordo ("Fat Hill") on the western slopes of the Inyo Mountains, and for the ten years of their most productive life, the Cerro Gordo mines sent about $8 million worth of ore over primitive wagon roads down the Owens Valley and the Mojave Desert, through Cajon Pass, then on to Los Angeles for shipment via the coast to refineries in northern California.

Even while great numbers of "single-blanket jackass prospectors," as they were popularly described, scrambled around in the old mountains looking for the romance of gold and silver, a big business was developing in something a good deal more banal—borate mining. In 1862, John and Dennis Searles, who had joined the French expedition in search of the Lost Gunsight Mine, discovered borate deposits of unusual purity in a huge dry lake bed on the plain between the Slate Range and the El Paso Mountains, and by the end of the 1870s the Searles brothers' San Bernardino Borax Mining Company was one of the biggest industries in Southern California, hauling enormous wagonloads of borate ore out of Searles Lake down to the town of Mojave, seventy-five miles away, where the Southern Pacific Railroad's line came down out of the Tehachapi Mountains on its way to points east. In the 1880s, similar borate operations were supplanting the mining of silver and copper at Calico in the center of the Mojave Desert, and even bigger borate mines were developed in Death Valley itself, where the

Harmony Borax Works and Eagle Borax Works dredged dry lake beds and tunneled into the mountains after the stuff with great success until they (like almost all the desert's borate enterprises) were folded into F. M. "Borax" Smith's monopoly, the Pacific Coast Borax Company, whose twenty-mule teams became both a trademark of the company and an emblem of the Old West.

Still, the dream of gold and silver (and sometimes copper and other semiprecious ores by now) would not die, and it set in motion a boom-and-bust cycle in one district that was remarkable even for an industry whose history had been written in such cataclysmic fluctuations. In the 1890s, gold was discovered in a related cluster of hills that included the El Paso Mountains, the Lava Mountains, Red Mountain, and a low-lying range that was called the Rand Mountains. The latter name was inspired by the famous gold mining district of South Africa, much in the news in the 1890s, and the imitative spirit continued when the biggest mine in the complex was called the Rand Mine, the biggest town Randsburg, and its nearest neighbor, Johannesburg (called "Jo'burg" by its denizens). The district produced approximately $3 million in gold, but by the first years of the twentieth century its mines were nearly exhausted. Then tungsten was discovered in the area and when World War I exploded, the consequent demand for the metal brought another boom—at least until the end of the war, after which an enormous drop in tungsten prices almost depopulated the district. For a few months, in any case—for in 1919 a major deposit of silver was discovered at Red Mountain not far from the original gold mining areas, and by 1926 the California Rand Silver Company had produced more than $13 million worth. Three years later, the deposit was so worked out that the company sold its property for $50,000, and nothing more that was newsworthy ever again came out of the last true mining boom area of the California Desert.

THERE WOULD BE ONLY ONE MORE gold strike of any size to speak of before World War II—at Soledad Mountain near Mojave, where the Gold Queen Mine was discovered in 1933—and that remained a single-owner operation of minor importance. By the end of the war, such excitements were the stuff of legend, although there would always be a population of starry-eyed hopefuls out scouring the

gullies and gulches of the desert, not a few of them of the "single-blanket jackass" variety. (Today, of course, the average prospector is more likely to be powered by four-wheel, not four-legged, drive). By any fair measure, the mining frenzies of the nineteenth and early twentieth centuries produced relatively little in the way of treasure; U.S. Bureau of Mine estimates place the total value of gold and silver taken out of the California Desert between the era of the gold rush and 1981 at about $1.5 billion in 1979 dollars — an average of just a shade over $1 million a year — and since most of the production of these two minerals took place when the price of both gold and silver was but a fraction of 1979 prices, the value in real dollars was hundreds of millions less. Their only enduring contribution to the national patrimony has been a colorful folklore and the artifacts that

accompany it — thousands of prospecting and mining sites sprinkled throughout the desert and windy little ghost towns like Calico and Ballarat, many of which attract tens of thousands of sight-seers annually.

In the end, it was not mining — not even the big corporate operations in borate, pumice, talc, and potash that developed during the war years — nor the ranching and small farming enter-prises which grew up to meet the industry's needs that gave the California Desert its most significant economic development. After the completion of the Colorado River Project in the 1930s and early 1940s, with Hoover, Parker, Davis, and Imperial dams to provide flood control, power generation, and — especially — irrigation, agriculture on a mas-sive scale blossomed in the floodplain of the Colorado — the old homeland of the long-

More thwarted enterprise: a sulphur mine in the Last Chance Range, abandoned after an explosion in the 1940s ripped most of it to flinders. (Suzi Moore)

During the heyday of mining in the latter nineteenth and early twentieth centuries, there were an astonishing number of little railroads in the California Desert—among them the California Southern, the Daggett & Borate, and the Tonopah & Tidewater. This tiny locomotive, *Emil,* serviced one of the smallest of them all—the Waterloo Mine Company railway operating out of Calico. (Courtesy of the Bancroft Library, University of California, Berkeley)

Many desert mining operations in the nineteenth century were of the family variety, although the women shown here at the Sue Mine in the Calico Mountains look a little out of place in their dirndls and aprons. (Courtesy of the Bancroft Library, University of California, Berkeley)

vanquished Mojave Indians—and on an even more extraordinary scale in the Imperial and Coachella valleys below and above the Salton Sea. Such river towns as Needles and Blythe grew like the cotton fields and melon plantations and oceans of lettuce the Colorado's water nourished, as did the desert hamlets of the Salton Sink, especially Brawley, El Centro and Indio. During the war, the agricultural population boom was more than matched by one that took place in the Mojave Desert, as big military installations like Edwards and George Air Force bases, the marine training station above Twentynine Palms, and other complexes demanded substantial urban growth to house civilian support staff and families and provide necessary services for them and for military personnel. Villages like Barstow, Victorville, Lancaster, and Palmdale became towns and finally cities.

The shape of the future had been established. The postwar economic boom and the Cold War—"the peace of mutual terror," Sir Winston Churchill called it—assured that the growth of the war years would continue, and it took on new impetus with the construction of major freeway systems that enabled hundreds of thousands of people to live in the pure air and open spaces of the desert while commuting to their jobs in the increasingly fetid atmosphere of the San Bernardino Valley and even the Los Angeles Basin. Real estate had come to the California Desert, adding one more pressure to all the rest that were beginning to imperil the integrity of a land that, in spite of the weight of history, had so far retained much of the beauty, distance, and lovely solitude that had driven John C. Van Dyke to an overwhelming starburst of prose in 1901:

In sublimity—the superlative degree of beauty— what land can equal the desert with its wide plains, its grim mountains, and its expanding canopy of sky! You shall never see elsewhere as here the dome, the pinnacle, the minaret fretted with golden fire at sunrise and sunset; you shall never see elsewhere as here the sunset valleys swimming in a pink and lilac haze, the great mesas and plateaus fading into blue distance, the gorges and canyons banked full of purple shadow. Never again shall you see such light and air and color; never such opaline mirage, such rosy dawn, such fiery twilight. And wherever you go, by land or by sea, you shall not forget that which you saw not but rather felt—the desolation and the silence of the desert.

Putting a woman on an ore bucket was one of the oldest photographic tricks in the nineteenth-century mining West—a gimmick repeated here at one of the more primitive operations in the Randsburg District. (Courtesy of the Bancroft Library, University of California, Berkeley)

Walter Scott, born in Kentucky around 1870, joined Buffalo Bill's Wild West Show then came to the California Desert in search of a lost mine. He found no mine, but he did find millionaire Albert Johnson, who built this winter retreat and installed Scott as a kind of caretaker and general factotum. The old prospector lived here even after Death Valley became a national monument—so long, in fact, that the Johnson retreat became known as "Scotty's Castle." It is the valley's most-visited tourist attraction today. (T. H. Watkins)

THE PLACE
2. The Heart of Mojave

SOUTH OF DEATH VALLEY, occupying about 260,000 acres of desert just below that point where the briney Amargosa River turns northwest, is the Kingston Range. Taken by themselves, these mountains offer an uncommonly diverse collection of landscape types and the vegetation and animal life (including human) that go with them. Elevations range from sand dunes a few hundred feet above sea level to rock-ribbed mountains as high as 7,300 feet — where white fir, a rarity anywhere in the desert, can be found above stands of juniper and piñon pine. The mountains harbor bands of desert bighorn sheep and rock-scrambling backpackers, while riparian areas along the Amargosa River, Horsethief Springs, and Salt Creek attract uncommon numbers of vermilion flycatchers, yellow-billed cuckoos, and bird-watchers. There are desert pupfish and prairie falcons, desert tortoises and Panamint chipmunks, hikers and bikers.

The Kingston Range is a popular place for desert-lovers, and because of that it illustrates an important point. For the purposes of this book, we are calling the California Desert an island; while the description is indisputably loose, it is a convenient way of describing the region's unique character as a still-wild place surrounded on almost all sides by the trappings of civilization. But it might be even more suggestive (if equally inaccurate geographically) to say that the desert is a collection of islands within an island, a place where one can find enclaves like the Kingston Range, small enough to be explored and experienced in a matter of days, but at the same time large enough to provide the sense of space, solitude, and diversity that is the essence of the desert.

There are many such generally self-contained enclaves in the desert, but it would be difficult to find one outside Death Valley or Joshua Tree national monuments that offers more in the way of accessible variety and open space than an 800,000-acre chunk of land wedged between Interstate 15 in the north, Interstate 40 on the south, the Nevada border and the Piute Valley on the east, and the Bristol Mountains on the west. The Bureau of Land Management calls this enormous region the East Mojave National Scenic Area and manages it as a single unit — a logic roundly applauded by conservationists, who view it not only as one of the BLM's primary treasures but as a place that presents the nation with one of its rarest and happiest opportunities: the chance to create a spanking-new national park, one that in size and diversity would match either of the national monuments (though there exists a powerful sentiment to enlarge both the monuments and reclassify *them* as national parks, too).

As we will shortly see, this notion of a Mojave National Park has its opponents, not the least important of whom is the BLM, which is in no particular hurry to turn over so large and attractive a piece of its property to the National Park Service. Nevertheless, there is a genuine movement afoot, and even the briefest survey of the territory under consideration here goes a long way toward explaining why those who *do* want this to become a national park want it passionately — and often at the top of their lungs.

Sunset-lit jumble of the Granite Mountains, East Mojave. (Suzi Moore)

Looking up into the
New York Mountains
from the floor of
Carruthers Canyon.
(T. H. Watkins)

IKE MANY EXISTING NATIONAL PARKS, IT IS not an entirely unroaded wilderness, the East Mojave—though to dignify many of its tracks by calling them roads would be stretching logic; most of this country is a place for the four-wheeled or even two-legged beast (and if conservationists are listened to, much of it deservedly would be protected from four-wheelers entirely). Still, three main routes cross the region from north to south between Interstate 15, the high road to Las Vegas from the Los Angeles Basin, and its twin to the south, Interstate 40, which leads on to the unglittered city of Kingman. All three cross-Mojave routes are paved in greater or lesser degree, and even their unpaved portions tend to be decently graded dirt or gravel easily traveled by regular vehicle except in the rainiest weather. More important, each provides access to agreeably primitive side roads that lead to the best of what the East Mojave has to offer in the way of adventure, beauty, and what E. B. White once called "the jewel of loneliness."

The westernmost route—called Kelbaker Road—begins at Baker and wanders past the western end of an ancient lava bed, through the shallow valley between the Marl Mountains and the Kelso Mountains, then directly south through the old railhead of Kelso and past the Kelso Dunes on its way to a meeting with Interstate 40 at a point just south of the Granite Mountains. Southwest of its upper stem is Soda Lake, a playa in the "floodplain" of the Mojave River, which at this point is just a wide, dry wash—except that every twenty years or so it does indeed flood, filling the lake bed as in the days of its Pleistocene past; the last time it did so was in 1969. East of Soda Lake is Old Dad Mountain, a steep-sided rocky eminence in a range that is home to what is probably the biggest aggregation of bighorn sheep in the East Mojave—as many as three hundred animals, according to estimates of the California Department of Fish & Game—and just southwest of Old Dad Mountain is the Devils Playground, a peaceful expanse of gently rolling hills covered with sand and various desert shrubs.

The sand that cloaks the Devils Playground is blown here mostly from the San Bernardino Mountains to the west. This same source provides most of the basic material that goes into one of the East Mojave's best-known attractions just south of the Playground—the Kelso Dunes, which at five to six hundred feet are second in height only to the Eureka Dunes north of Death

Valley. The wind that brings the sand here meets local winds that come at it from all points of the compass; the result is a spinning tempest of air that often is marked by dune grasses whose wind-blown tips have drawn nearly perfect circles in the sand—a photographer's delight. On occasions when the air is still and the temperature is right and some force like a human foot has caused sand to break from its angle of repose and slide down the face of a pyramid, the dunes will sing to you, as the grains of quartz and feldspar rub against one another to produce what one entranced listener, travel writer Suzanne Venino, has described as a "low, resonant" sound "like the notes of an organ."

Not far from the dunes is the village of Kelso, a former stop on the still-functioning Union Pacific line across the desert. Its station, built in the 1920s, is no longer in use, but is in fair condition and is too fine a specimen of depot architecture to be razed; plans are underway to restore it as a historic site. Rising in a long, gray line ten miles to the east of Kelso—and visible throughout most of the whole western third of the East Mojave—are the Providence Mountains, some of whose peaks top out at more than 7,000 feet and whose slopes boast barrel cacti six feet high, as well as populations of bighorn sheep and even mule deer. Portions of the range are laced by extensive limestone cave systems, chief among them the Mitchell Caverns Natural Preserve, part of the Providence Mountains State Recreation Area on the eastern side of the mountains.

On the western side of Granite Pass at the southern foot of the Providence Mountains lie the Granite Mountains—or, more accurately, *one* set of Granite Mountains, for there are a number of similarly-named ranges scattered throughout southern California. These, within sight of Interstate 40, feature ring-tailed cats and bighorn sheep, among other animals, as well as towering piles of huge rocks that are extensively used in the practice of the increasingly popular branch of the sport of rock climbing called boulder scrambling or bouldering; on any given weekend, the mountains are likely to be ornamented with little clots of adventurers who attempt to emulate bighorn sheep (which, for their part, tend to leave the neighborhood, possibly in disgust).

The second route across the East Mojave is called the Cima Road and begins at a junction with Interstate 15 a little over seven miles east of Halloran Summit. The road, which is paved throughout its length, does not go all the way

Sedimentary rock is twisted up into an uncommonly obvious syncline in Woods Wash. (Jim Dodson/California Desert Protection League)

Moonscape from the Soda Mountains, looking down on Soda Lake on the northwestern edge of East Mojave. (Elden Hughes/California Desert Protection League)

across, but ends at Kelso after passing down the wide Shadow Valley beneath the Ivanpah Mountains to the hamlet of Cima, then curving southwest past the Mid Hills Range to its junction with the Kelbaker Road. Along the way, it passes within striking distance of two of the East Mojave's chief attractions. The first of these are the rolling hills just southwest of the Shadow Valley, remarkable for an ancient Joshua tree forest that contains an estimated 325,000 trees, at least 25,000 of which are five hundred or more years old. The second, just to the south of the Joshua forest, is a huge volcanic blister of land called the Cima Dome, a geological oddity covered by juniper and Joshua trees and thick undergrowth featuring three major species of yucca and several of cholla cactus; parts of the dome have been administratively designated by the BLM both as Natural Area and "Outstanding" Natural Area, and the region as a whole currently is under study as an addition to the National Natural Landmark system.

The eastern third of the East Mojave is bisected by a route that does go all the way across the Scenic Area, although this one is graded dirt for roughly half its fifty-mile length. It begins at a junction with the Nipton Road three and a half miles east of that point where Interstate 15 turns sharply north in the direction of Las Vegas; from there, on a short paved segment, it goes through

Looking north across the wind-whipped Kelso Dunes toward the Kelso Mountains, East Mojave. (Terrence Moore)

Rainstorm at sunrise, the Kelso Dunes, East Mojave. (Terrence Moore)

The rays of the morning sun illuminate the confusion of stone called the Granite Mountains, East Mojave. (Terrence Moore)

the abandoned town of Ivanpah before becoming graded dirt and starting to climb through a narrow pass that cuts across the New York Mountains; once through the pass, it cuts a nearly straight path south through the wide Lanfair Valley, past the Grotto Hills, the Lanfair Buttes, Hackberry Mountain, and the Vontrigger Hills before reaching the town of Goffs at the Scenic Area's southern border six miles above Interstate 40. In the hundreds of square miles on either side of the route, there are landscapes of uncluttered beauty, ecologically important nooks and crannies, and even some gentle reminders of the length of time humans have been present in this land.

To the southwest of the pass that begins just below Ivanpah, the rocky band of the New York Mountains begins a long, ragged climb that extends forty miles and reaches an altitude of

more than 7,500 feet. Like the Granite Mountains to the southwest, the New York Mountains are marked by the presence of buff-colored and jointed granitic rocks that have been so fractured and tumbled about by time, erosion, and geological movement that they mount up in huge complexes of boulders—less well-known for scrambling purposes, but no less challenging. Unlike the Granite Mountains—or any other region of the East Mojave—the slopes and canyons of these mountains harbor an extraordinary mix of vegetation.

There are estimated to be at least 288 individual plant species in the New York Mountains—not only the standard desert types, but such exotics as a relict stand of 30 white fir trees in Fourth of July Canyon, as well as examples of coastal chaparral that survive from the

era 10,000 or more years ago, when the climate was wetter and more temperate: manzanita, California lilac, silk tassel, oak, and yerba santa, any or all of which can be found in sites like Caruthers Canyon.

On the northeastern side of the pass below Ivanpah, the mountains rise to another kind of rarity—Castle Buttes, a set of redrock volcanic spires that jut more than 600 feet above the surrounding landscape not far from the Nevada border. "If you really want to get away from it all," Lynn Foster writes in *Adventuring in the California Desert* (Sierra Club Books), which stands unchallenged as the best guide to the region, "Castle Buttes country is about as far away and as unpopulated a place as you'll find in the California Desert."

A few miles south of the New York Moun-

tains, lifting 2,000 feet above the western floor of the Lanfair Valley, is Table Top Mountain, a 10,000-acre movie-set mesa that looks as if it had been taken in one piece out of Arizona's Monument Valley and put down here in a place where such tableland monoliths are a rare sight. Farther down that side of the Lanfair Valley are the Woods Mountains, which, among other things, offer some of the most extensive cactus gardens anywhere in the California Desert, with mixtures of barrel, cholla, prickly pear, beavertail, and the uncommon old-man cactus; the mountains also contain three known golden eagle eyries. A little to the southeast, in the region around Hackberry Mountain at the southern end of the valley, are about twelve square miles of permanent and seasonal range for a band of twenty-one bighorn sheep.

Cholla garden in the Dead Mountains above the Colorado River, East Mojave. (Suzi Moore)

Barrel cacti and
boulders in the Granite
Mountains, East Mojave.
(Terrence Moore)

Snowstorm atop the mound of Cima Dome, East Mojave. (Jim Dodson/California Desert Protection League)

A springtime scene in the Joshua tree forest of Cima Dome, East Mojave. (Dean Slaughter/California Desert Protection League)

49

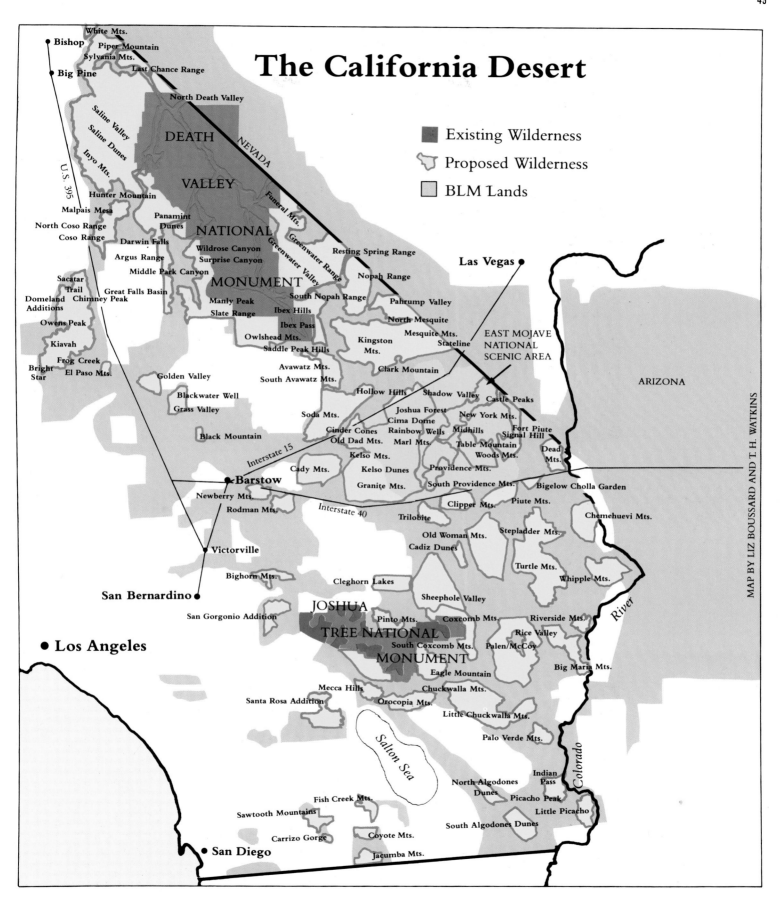

The California Desert

- Existing Wilderness
- Proposed Wilderness
- BLM Lands

MAP BY LIZ BOUSSARD AND T. H. WATKINS

Winter scene looking
toward the New York
Mountains from Cima
Dome, East Mojave.
(Jim Dodson/California
Desert Protection
League)

Thirty miles to the east across the broad, arid valley lies the Piute Range, which marks the eastern boundary of the Scenic Area. This long, low wall of mountains overlooks the Piute Valley, which is bordered on its eastern side by the Dead Mountains, where Mojave legend said the god Mastamho built his house. The Piute Range itself also was considered holy, for it was a narrow, rock-ribbed pass in the heart of the range that connected the Mojave to a long trading route to the coast that had been established perhaps hundreds of years before European contact—as numerous petroglyphs around Piute Spring just above the pass would indicate. The trading route, which crossed the Lanfair Valley and the New York Mountains, entered the wide wash of the Mojave River, then tracked its way west across the Mojave to Cajon Pass, became a common route of the Spanish between Arizona and California and was followed by the Americans after the Mexican War. Traffic was especially heavy during the Civil War years, when wagonloads of supplies were hauled from the coast to the scattered civilian settlements and military posts of New Mexico Territory (which at that

time included what is now Arizona); the ruins of Fort Piute, a tiny military post built in those years to protect the route from Indian irritations, can still be seen near Piute Spring—cheek-by-jowl, as it were, with the relics of the generations of Indians who had come before. The Mojave Road, as it was by then known, fell into disuse after railroad connections to the east were established in the 1870s and 1880s, but a century later the Friends of the Mojave Road, an energetic bunch of four-wheel-drive enthusiasts, have retraced much of it in the hope of making it a permanent part of the desert experience. "The Mojave is a natural and cultural museum," one of the friends declares, "and the Mojave Road is an 8-foot-wide, 138-mile-long artifact."

But elsewhere in the East Mojave—indeed, in the rest of the California Desert—both natural and historical artifacts are not always so lovingly regarded. Nor, some would say, is the Bureau of Land Management, the desert's proprietor, temperamentally or administratively prepared to give the land the protection it must have if it is to survive the worst of what we can do to it by using it up or loving it to death.

Table Mountain as seen from the floor of the Lanfair Valley, East Mojave. (Elden Hughes/California Desert Protection League)

The Signal Hills above the Lanfair Valley, East Mojave. (Elden Hughes/California Desert Protection League)

Critters

ESERT IS A PLACE FOR ADAPTA-
tions. It does not preclude life, but it
demands of it special effort, and the
creatures that have evolved to make
their home in a land of little rain, sparse
and less-than-succulent vegetation,
sand, stone, and profound changes in
temperature during the course of any
given day are consequently tougher than
they are numerous.

Consider, for instance, the kangaroo rat, a
nocturnal creature eminently fitted for life in the
desert because it subsists entirely without drink-
ing; it gets all the water it needs from the chemis-
try of converting food (seeds and some greens)
to energy and by oxidizing the fat in its body—

moreover, it has no sweat glands and it concen-
trates its urine and its feces before elimination.
Four individual species of kangaroo rat are known
to occur in the area embraced by the California
Desert, but only two—Merriam's kangaroo rat
(*Dipodomys merriami*) and the desert kangaroo rat
(*Dipodomys deserti*)—range throughout the entire
region. They are particularly fond of dune systems, which provide them with deep, relatively
cool daytime burrows, and where the animals'
tracks can be found almost any morning, like tiny
petroglyphs, marking their passage through the
night.

Or, at the other end of the scale, consider
the desert pupfish (*Cyprinodon macularius*), which,
obviously enough, is utterly dependent upon
water but is no less a uniquely desert creature than
the kangaroo rat. This tiny fish—which is found
primarily in the Salton Sea region and may be
descended from populations that once lived in
Pleistocene seas—thrives in waters too salty, alka-
line, or warm to support any other kind of fish.

Between the waterless kangaroo rat and the
warm-water pupfish is a biological spectrum
occupied by a wide variety of creatures that swim,
walk, crawl, and fly here as they do nowhere else,
adapting and multiplying as the desert demands
and the human population allows. One of the
most ubiquitous is the desert tortoise, though
it is getting less ubiquitous with every passing
year, as highway traffic, lost habitat, and mindless killing take their toll of the big, lumbering
reptiles; current estimates put the number of
tortoises—which once ran to the millions—at
somewhere between 300,000 and 1,000,000. (In

A desert bighorn ram in
the Kingston Mountains.
(Mike McWherter/
California Desert
Protection League)

The desert tortoise is too easy and too
frequent a target for speeding automobiles
and is equally threatened by the destruction
of its habitat. (Terrence Moore)

A splendid portrait of the definitive desert critter—the chuckwalla. (Elden Hughes/California Desert Protection League)

the *Audubon Wildlife Report* for 1988/89, Faith Thompson Campbell of the Natural Resources Defense Council warns that both figures may be too high, for "BLM's population maps . . . make no allowance for extensive areas of human disturbance within the tortoise's range.") If the tortoise is ubiquitous, the desert bighorn sheep (*Ovis canadensis*) is nearly invisible, being an exceedingly shy creature that travels in small bands; possibly *because* of their retiring disposition (as well as the fact that there was a ban on hunting them in California for nearly a century, and even today hunting is severely restricted), it is estimated that some 5,000 of these beautiful sheep survive in many of the desert's higher mountain ranges, such as the Providence Mountains, the New York Mountains, or the Kingston Range.

This is coyote country, of course, and there are plenty of the wide-ranging old "song dogs"

(*Canis latrans*) to be found—although trapping, hunting, and poisoning programs have all but eliminated them from various ranching areas. The desert is lizard country, too, and the tribe is well represented—there are geckos (*Coleonyx brevis*), Mojave fringe-toed lizards (*Uma scoparia*), black-collared lizards (*Crotaphytus insularis*), and thirteen additional species—among the biggest, and by far the most colorful, of which is the chuckwalla (*Sauromalus obesus*)—a fat (as the Linnaean Latin would suggest), potbellied creature that can reach lengths of ten or eleven inches.

And then there are the birds who live in, or at least pass through, the desert in numbers

A sidewinder, coiled and ready in the Riverside Mountains. (Edward S. Ross/California Desert Protection League)

When it emerges from its cocoon, this gorgeous caterpillar will become the even more striking short-tailed black swallowtail butterfly, common in most of the desert. (Edward S. Ross/California Desert Protection League)

The desert raven, like the chuckwalla, is one of the desert's most ubiquitous creatures. It also preys on young tortoises when their shells are still tender, making it one more in a bundle of threats the hapless tortoise must face. (Mike McWherter/ California Desert Protection League)

Golden eagle in a Joshua
tree on Cima Dome.
(Suzi Moore)

that belie the scarcity of water and riparian habitat. The raptors are represented by the golden eagle, almost as ubiquitous as the desert tortoise, and numerous species of hawks—many of them, like Cooper's hawk (*Accipiter cooperii*), found throughout most of the United States but others, like Harris' hawk (*Parabuteo unicinctus*), confined in this country to the lower Colorado River Valley and other parts of the Sonoran Desert. Common barn owls (*Tyto alba*) and great horned owls (*Bubo virginianus*) wing the night in search of kangaroo rats, while among the less predatory species are the topknotted California quail (*Callipepla californica*), the mourning dove (*Zenaida macroura*), as common as the city pigeon (though a good deal less arrogant), and the white-winged dove (*Zenaida asiatica*), found only in the southern part of the desert; and a splendid assortment of songbirds, from the hooded oriole (*Icterus cucullatus*) to the blue grosbeak (*Guiraca caerulea*).

THE PROBLEM

WITNESSED MY FIRST AND ONLY desert motorcycle race more than twenty years ago, and the experience moved me to set down what I had seen and heard in the little conservation magazine *Cry California*. The piece has since been anthologized a number of times and is worth repeating here for its shock value, if nothing else, and to demonstrate just how old an old fight can get:

Silence is perhaps the most impressive thing that the desert has to offer. There are sounds, of course—the chattering of birds, the muted rattling of mesquite and needle grass touched by the wind, the rustling of small animals. Yet these sounds only serve to emphasize the vastness of the desert's essential silence—a stillness that emphasizes the enormity of the space that surrounds you. It is incredibly beautiful, this delicate collaboration between space and silence; you do not shout, for fear that the sound will shatter the balance and go sweeping across the bleak country like fire in a tinder-dry forest.

Suddenly, you hear a low rumbling. You look to the mountains, but there are no clouds to indicate a distant storm. The birds have stopped singing. A scrubby little desert rabbit skitters from behind a clump of creosote bush and heads off across the desert floor. He is followed by several others. A terrified coyote joins them. The rumble has by now become a dull, steady thundering.

And then, on the crest of the horizon, you see them.

Motorcyclists, hundreds of them, too many to count, too many to believe. They are strung across the landscape like some grotesque re-enactment of the Oklahoma land rush, bounding over rocks, grinding through sand washes, flattening bushes, leaping arroyos, challenging the cracks and lumps and dangers of the land in a frenzied game of hares and

hounds. Behind them, a dust cloud a mile wide and a hundred feet high billows into the flat blue sky. As they reach and pass you, the sound is a scream and bellow that pummels your eardrums and shakes the ground beneath your feet. Helmeted and goggled, their faces begrimed, they race remorselessly on, until they are dimmed by the dust and distance, and their sound declines once again to a rumble, a whisper, and finally to nothing.

The air reeks of gasoline, oil, burned rubber, and the heavy smell of exhaust fumes. You walk across the path the motorcycles have taken and note what they have left behind: shrubs and grass and cacti mutilated, the earth itself maimed and rutted by hundreds of tire tracks. In an hour or so, the wind will clean the air of the dust and the stench, but nothing can be done to repair the earth, or to muffle the pounding roar that continues to echo in your mind.

It was the 167-mile Barstow-to-Vegas race, a desert tradition since 1967, and by the early 1970s the hundreds of participants I had seen in 1968 had grown to as many as 3,000, whose machines were scarring hundreds of thousands of acres of land so little equipped to reclaim itself that the tracks left behind by General George Patton's tank corps during Mojave Desert training exercises in 1942 could still be seen (and can still be seen today). In 1974, responding to conservationist pressure and its own best instincts, the Bureau of Land Management banned the Barstow-to-Vegas race on the grounds that it was too damaging to the land to be tolerated. In 1983, in spite

A cycler tests the slopes of Jawbone Canyon, one of many large areas the BLM has allotted for the sport of dirt-bike hill climbing and other popular off-road vehicle adventures. (Terrence Moore)

Dirt bikers in the Dove Spring area of the East Mojave National Scenic Area. (Terrence Moore)

of conservationist pressure and its own best instincts, the agency reauthorized the race — limiting participation to 1,200 bikers — and every year since then hundreds of modern dirt bikes have gone screaming across the desert from the vicinity of Barstow to Kactus Kate's casino at Stateline, Nevada — not quite Vegas, but close enough for promotion purposes. In 1988 the race course was rerouted slightly to keep the cycles out of Soda Lake in the northwestern corner of the East Mojave National Scenic Area — although the new route included twenty-two miles of previously unscarred desert through the Soda Mountains and Hollow Hills segments of the area. Conservationists, who had objected to the race every year with growing intensity, were unimpressed by the limit on participants and were no more pleased with the new route than with the old, pointing out that it included at least two miles of critical desert-tortoise habitat and nine archaeological sites. BLM spokesmen said that the riders would confine themselves to existing gravel roads in the area. "There's absolutely no way they can really do any damage up there," a BLM recreation planner stoutly told a reporter.

Patricia Schifferle, The Wilderness Society's regional representative for California, was not convinced. "In every single one of these," she told the same reporter, "there's always straying, there's always, 'Oops, sorry, that won't happen again.'"

"The race should not be run at all," added Elden Hughes, director of the California Desert Protection League. "It's going to trash a lot of areas that are not disturbed. It's going to have an enormous impact on the visual quality of the desert."

The race was run, and while interested parties in the months that followed attempted to assess the impact on the land, protagonists and antagonists gathered their forces and their arguments for another round of increasingly bitter debate in a struggle that is now approaching the quarter-century mark and may or may not find a solution in the windy caverns of the United States Congress.

At issue is the question of the public use of public lands. "The public has to make a choice," a former BLM employee told local journalist Cathy Armstrong in January of 1988. "Is it going to be managed for multiple use and sustained yield, or is it going to be managed to preserve scenery and wildlife, to leave it unimpaired for future generations?" (One might remind him that scenery and wildlife are properly included as multiple uses in the correct interpretation of the term.) The question is not unique to the California Desert — though, like the serrated edges of the desert's mountain ranges, it tends to stand out here in stark relief. So will any resolution that may come, for decisions made in regard to this great desert island inevitably will have a profound effect on similar decisions yet to be made in other public land states, where the future of millions of acres has yet to be determined. It is one more twist on Richard Armour's old ironic quatrain —

So jump with joy, be blithe and gay,
Or weep, my friends, in sorrow;
What California is today,
The rest will be tomorrow.

The enormity of the problem cannot be escaped, for the pressures on the desert come at it from a bewildering number of directions with a bewildering number of objectives behind them, some of them mutually exclusive. Begin with population pressures. According to statistics presented in Armstrong's feature story in the January 10, 1988, *San Bernardino Sun,* the region's largest newspaper, as many as 17 million people live within a few hours' drive of the desert, a number that is expected to bloat to more than 23 million in the next twenty years or so. Almost a million people live in desert communities today — and that number is expected to top 1.4 million in the same twenty years. There are no

firm figures available for the number of recreationists out of all these millions who visit the desert each year, the newspaper noted, but an informal poll taken in 1977 suggested that it may have been as many as 7 million people a year then and it could only have risen since. Nor are the recreationists—however many they may be—all cut from the same cloth. At one extreme are the hikers and backpackers and climbers whose delight is to get in and out of the land with the power of their own feet; there are hundreds of thousands of them, at least, whose interests are represented (even if not all of them are members) by hiking and climbing clubs and such environmental groups as the Angeles Chapter of the Sierra Club, The California/Nevada regional office of The Wilderness Society, and the California Desert Protection League. At the other extreme are those who take their joy behind the handlebars or steering wheels of as many as 1 million motorcycles, dirt bikes, three- and four-wheel ATVs (all-terrain vehicles), dune buggies, and four-wheel drive trucks and jeeps; there are at least hundreds of thousands of them, too, whose interests are represented (even if not all of them are members) by small clubs and societies and by such large organizations as the American Motorcycle Association and the California Association of Four-Wheel Drive Clubs. As the contretemps over the Barstow-to-Vegas race suggests, there often is little room for agreement between these two aggregations of desert users.

A herd of all-terrain vehicles returns from the Algodones Dunes, a popular spot for dirt sports. (Terrence Moore)

Every year, tens of thousands of RV owners gather at Furnace Creek for the annual Death Valley Encampment; the parking-lot vista here was photographed in November 1988. (T. H. Watkins)

An ATV rider sends up a plume of dust in the Algodones Dunes. (Terrence Moore)

The millions of recreationists who occupy the middle portion of the spectrum use the desert perhaps less frequently and less dramatically than either of these extremes, but use it they do—for camping, picknicking, occasional rockhounding or bottle collecting, general sightseeing, and just gadding about in one of the few places left to them where time is allowed to stand still for at least a while.

To satisfy present transportation needs (including those of all brands of recreationists), the desert already is latticed by more than 2,500 miles of freeways and highways and by another 40,000 miles of lesser roads and trails. Some 12,000 miles are crisscrossed by oil and gas pipelines, 3,500 miles by power lines. At least 100 microwave towers, all of them seemingly painted the same startling white, dot the peaks and shoulders of the mountains, looking for all the world like space-age hardware abandoned on the moon.

There are less austere marks of technology to be found in the desert. In addition to many thousands of abandoned mines, there are additional thousands of pending, unworked mining claims—many of them decades, even generations, old—in the 11.5 million acres of publicly owned desert land that is open to extraction, and, according to a 1986 analysis by The Wilderness Society's resource geologist, Thomas Goerold, 123 active mines are busily digging out everything from gold to tungsten. Some of these are open-pit operations of respectable dimensions, including a 2,320-acre borate facility at Boron and a 6,415-acre saline works at Searles Lake. The mining industry says that it sees in the years ahead opportunities for growth in the region. The BLM tends to agree. Conservationists tend to disagree.

The military, which already uses its 3 million acres to test rocket engines, land and launch supersonic aircraft, receive returning space shuttles, engage in bombing and gunnery practice, train pilots in high-speed, low-level flight maneuvers, and run tanks and half-tracks and jeeps and trucks and artillery and rocket launchers and marines across the land in the hugely complex and messy exercises called war games, would like to have some more desert. Specifically, the army has been considering asking Congress to add another 200,000 acres of previously unexercised land to the 635,000 acres of its Fort Irwin National Training Center so that it can expand its war maneuvers to brigade size.

Such, in brutally brief outline, are some of the forces that will, one way or another, change

Bouldering is one of the most popular of the non-wheeled desert sports. This triumphant gaggle of climbers was photographed in the Stepladder Mountains. (Bob Emerick/California Desert Protection League)

the face of the California Desert in the decades to come. Some have pretty firm ideas of what that face should be.

TO GIVE THE BLM ITS DUE, THE AGENCY DID not just sit around waiting for things to happen as the growth in use and population began to affect the desert. "The BLM recognized the ORV [off-road vehicle] problem in the 1960s," Ed Hasty, the Bureau's director in Sacramento told Marc Reisner in the Winter 1986 issue of *Wilderness* magazine, for example. "We've been hard at work on this thing for twenty years. We recognize that they can injure desert values, and that's why we've excluded ORV use in many places." It was in 1968, in fact, that the California state office of the bureau and the western regional office of the National Park Service produced the first government report of any consequence on the impact of off-road vehicle use on public lands; the conclusion was that it was not good.

Still, it was not until the Federal Land Policy and Management Act (FLPMA) of 1976 was passed by Congress and signed into law by President Gerald Ford that any significant move began toward the development of a comprehensive plan for the future management of the BLM's portion of the California Desert. Among other things, the law mandated that the bureau survey all of its land in the contiguous forty-eight states to determine which portions of it might qualify for inclusion in the National Wilderness Preservation System, a network of federal wilderness areas where, in the words of the Wilderness Act of 1964, "the earth and its community of life are untrammeled by man, where man himself is a visitor who does not remain." In addition, in Section 601 of the FLPMA specifically called for the creation of a comprehensive management plan—including wilderness recommendations—for what it designated the "California Desert Conservation Area." This, of course, included the 12.1 million acres of BLM land, which the act, in an uncharacteristically poetic burst of language described as "a total ecosystem that is extremely fragile, easily scarred, and slowly healed."

With admirable enthusiasm, the Bureau's planners went to work, but it soon became apparent to interested conservation groups that the agency's commitment to the idea of wilderness preservation was not all that it might have been. In 1978, for instance, a number of groups objected when the bureau announced that it would not include in the system of wilderness study areas (WSAs) any area that had not, in its words, been "used for recreational purposes" in the past, as well as any area that lacked "physical screening"— which is to say, *shade*—"by topography or vegetation." These stipulations, critics pointed out, suggested that California's BLM office thought that the only true purpose of wilderness designation was its recreational value—a narrow-minded interpretation of the Wilderness Act's meaning that contradicted both the sentiment that had produced it and the manner in which it had

so far been implemented on other federal lands.

Unsurprisingly, then, the conservation community was neither surprised nor pleased by the *Final Environmental Impact Statement and Proposed Plan* for the CDCA (we will call it the California Desert Plan from this point forward) that the bureau issued and Interior Secretary Cecil Andrus approved in 1980. Out of about 5.7 million acres that could have been included in the National Wilderness Preservation System by accepted standards, the BLM recommended only 2.1 million, while offering to release most of the rest for other multiple-use purposes (mining, ranching, ORV use, general recreation, and virtually any other use to which the land conceivably could be put), and some of it for intensive use—large mining operations, wide areas turned over to off-road vehicles, and so on. Still, most of the conservation community decided that any plan was better than no plan at all, and hoped that it could persuade the BLM to implement this one very delicately until specific wilderness legislation could be formulated for consideration by Congress.

But in 1981, the Reagan administration entered the equation, with James Gaius Watt as secretary of the interior and Robert Burford as director of the Bureau of Land Management—both men constitutionally opposed to the whole idea of wilderness designation. From the point of view of conservationists, the situation began to deteriorate swiftly from an already unpromising beginning. The bureau cut its wilderness recommendation to 1.8 million acres, and Watt would have reduced that by another 150,000 acres if conservationists had not appealed the decision to the Interior Board of Land Appeals, over which Watt had no control. Furthermore, the BLM authorized no less than 550 actions on wilderness study areas between 1980 and 1986—including bulldozing, road building, water impoundment, cyanide storage for leach-mining purposes, ORV travel, exploratory drilling for minerals, and extensive excavations—this in spite of the fact that the FLPMA clearly stipulated that no development of any kind could take place on any WSA in the system that would in any way impair its suitability for wilderness designation.

By 1984, the Sierra Club, The Wilderness Society, and other critics of the bureau had seen enough. Terry Sopher, former head of the BLM's wilderness policy staff in Washington, D.C., but after 1981 director of BLM programs for The Wilderness Society, spoke with the anger of many

One of the least-known but growing desert enterprises is the "mining" of rocks displaying especially fine patinas of desert varnish, many of which end up in fireplaces. This bundled-up shipment was photographed near the Little Marias Mountains. (Terrence Moore)

Ranching is an increasingly scarce business on the California Desert, but some cattle still wander the landscape, competing with feral burros and bighorn sheep for the limited forage. The cows here are seen on Cima Dome. (Terrence Moore)

when he voiced his own: "Under the administration's policies, the management of the California Desert has been an utter failure," he said. "Other than the production of a big, thick document—the plan—the important job hasn't been done. The potential wilderness areas in the plan are being loaded up with destructive and incompatible uses. . . . In the vast majority of cases, they've approved these activities under a scandalous concept: they argue that it's okay to degrade existing wilderness values as long as you don't wreck the *entire* area. It's like saying you can scratch up one corner of a Picasso painting as long as you don't destroy it entirely."

Wilderness advocates began to work closely with California Senator Alan Cranston, a long-time environmentalist, and his staff to formulate wilderness legislation that would bypass the bureau's recommendations entirely. Over the next several months, as everyone from grass-roots field investigators to professional planners got a hand in, the legislation grew to become something infinitely more ambitious than one more wilderness bill—by the time Senator Cranston was ready to introduce his California Desert Protection Act for the first time early in 1986, it had become one of the most capacious, comprehensive, and carefully structured conservation documents since the revolutionary Alaska Lands Act of 1980.

For one thing, the California Desert Protection Act would have designated wilderness with a generous hand, 4.5 million acres of BLM wilderness alone: 16,100 acres of wilderness in the El Paso Mountains, 12,800 at Darwin Spring; 40,600 in the New York Mountains, 146,110 in the Old Woman Mountains; 75,640 in Owens Peak, 177,000 in the Sheephole Valley; 165,820 in the Kelso Dunes, 255,290 in the Kingston Range. On and on. . . . There would have been the Cima Dome Wilderness, the Rice Valley Wilderness, the Cleghorn Lakes Wilderness, the Whipple Mountains Wilderness, the Dead Mountains Wilderness, the Malpais Mesa Wilderness, the Chimney Peak Wilderness, the Golden Valley Wilderness—in all, eighty-four new wilderness areas for California, from Piper Mountain north of Death Valley to the Jacumba Mountains on the Mexican border.

But the bill did not stop with BLM wilderness. It would have added—as designated wilderness—the Saline and Eureka valleys, the Last Chance Range, an additional portion of the Funeral Mountains, the Greenwater Range, the

Panamint Dunes, and several other BLM areas to the present boundaries of Death Valley National Monument, would have designated other lands within the monument as wilderness, and would have reclassified the whole immense package as a national park. Down at the other end of the California Desert, the bill would have added—again, as designated wilderness—the Cottonwood Mountains, a portion of the Little San Bernardino Mountains, Eagle Mountain, the Coxcomb Mountains, and other BLM areas to Joshua Tree National Monument, and, just as at Death Valley, would have designated other lands within the monument as wilderness and would have made *it* a National Park.

The bill was not done yet. It would have taken the 1.5 million acres of East Mojave National Scenic Area away from the Bureau of Land Management and would have given them to the National Park Service as yet another brand-new national park. Furthermore, within this new national park it would have designated as wilderness nearly every portion in it that had not been roaded or otherwise seriously trammeled by man.

The subsequent uproar during 1986 was considerable, as opponents of wilderness rallied their arguments and began a systematic assault against the bill, while its proponents broadcast its virtues and defended it against its critics. The Bureau of Land Management, unsurprisingly, was not happy. Ed Hasty was particularly wounded, apparently, by the fact that Cranston's proposal did not pay tribute to the California Desert Plan, though one wonders what he could have expected. "The trouble with the Cranston proposal," he told conservation journalist Marc Reisner in the fall of 1986, "is it totally ignores the Desert Plan. We got 44,000 comments from citizens on our draft plan. Our Desert Advisory Committee was one of the best committees we've ever put together. We spent $8 million on the study. To ignore that whole process is just not fair and not right."

For her part, Marie Brashear, a small-time miner, rock hound, and four-wheel drive enthusiast from Riverside, helped to put together the California Desert Coalition, a collection of mining industries, ranchers, ORV users, and others with a stake against wilderness, for which she then went to work as its paid lobbyist. Her organization's argument, she explained to Reisner, was that the wilderness designations would eliminate vehicle access to most of the desert. "If this bill passes," she said, "a lot of the wilderness it

creates will never, ever be visited by human beings. . . . This whole idea is just a huge ego trip by environmentalists who want to see how much wilderness they can stuff under their belts."

When not busy stuffing wilderness, the environmentalists pointed out that each of the proposed wilderness areas was painstakingly "cherry-stemmed," drawn so that anything that could reasonably be described as a road—or even just a "way"—was excluded from the area's boundaries. "Even if we get every wilderness area in the Desert Protection Act approved," the Sierra Club's Jim Dodson claimed, "there'll still be something like 13,000 miles of paved and maintained dirt roads and 20,000 miles of routes and ways

open to motorized use." And it is true that the maps drawn to accompany the conservationist proposal are so full of excluded roads that "stems" of various lengths sprout from virtually every area outlined. A true purist might even argue that the "ego-ridden environmentalists" may have gone too far in their effort at compromise.

The second major criticism of the California Desert Protection Act came from the mining industry and its spokesmen—supported handsomely by the Bureau of Land Management. The argument here was that the act would lock up unknown billions of dollars worth of mineral resources, including rare earths and such strategic minerals as molybdenum, tungsten, and tho-

The sign on the gate of an obviously highly prized gold mining claim at Glamis, near the Algodones Dunes, makes an unintentional commentary on the conflicts that threaten the ecological well-being of the California Desert. (Suzi Moore)

rium, together with the jobs and local economic growth that would go with them. In 1986, Jim Dodson expressed the view that the lockup theory was spurious: "Other than gold, most of the minerals they're dragging out of the desert are things like borates, drilling muds, and talc. The hard-rock boom is probably played out forever, and when people talk about strategic minerals, in most cases they're talking about hard-rock minerals."

After a two-year study of the question, The Wilderness Society's Thomas Goerold would have refined that argument. "If you look at the region of the California Desert as a whole," he told me early in 1989, "I think you can say that mining for all kinds of things—including probably some strategic minerals—*is* going to remain an important part of the region's economy. What I find interesting, though," he added, "is the question of why the industry and the bureau are so agitated. Mining in these areas has been going on for a century. Wilderness advocates recognized that, and the proposed wilderness boundaries were consequently drawn very carefully to exclude the areas with mining."

Earlier, in March 1988, Goerold had challenged the mining industry's (and the BLM's) claim that supplies of rare earths—lanthanum and similar exotic elements that may (or may not, as technology improves) be used in high-temperature superconducting materials—would be threatened by wilderness designations. Present reserves, he had pointed out, were more than sufficient—there were enough rare earth oxides in the one operating rare earths mine, for example, to last the United States 254 years—and, he said, "it seems unnecessary to dig up the desert looking for more rare earth deposits if there's no demand for them." As for more mundane minerals, he pointed out to me later, only about 10 percent of currently active mines in the California Desert exist in, or even close to, any proposed wilderness. Finally, in regard to future development, he cited as an example an evaluation of the four largest wilderness study areas contained in *Mineral Summary for the California Desert Protection Act* (May 1988), a report prepared by the U.S. Geological Survey and the U.S. Bureau of Mines: the Saline Valley (486,300 acres), the Kingston Range (369,500 acres), the Palen/McCoy Mountains (225,300 acres), and the Turtle Mountains (189,300 acres). In every single case, the report determined that all of each of these areas was highly mineralized. Yet the

report's own geologist's maps for these wilderness study areas clearly indicated that the actual acreage within them that contained even moderate mineral potential (and all of this was educated guesswork, as such things always have been) was but a fraction of that removed from wilderness consideration—in the Saline Valley as the most egregious example, the fraction with any mineral potential was a little over two percent. As Goerold put it, "The government would have us throw out the baby with the bath water."

Goerold's logic may have been hard to dispute, but even if he had developed his figures early enough for them to have been factored into the debate in 1986, it is not likely they would have done much good. It usually takes the force of logic a long time to overcome the energy of passionate belief, and with Senator Pete Wilson refusing to join with Cranston in support of the bill and with a Congress forever reluctant to push wilderness legislation in any state without the

Some senior citizens enjoy a little hill climbing of their own at Furnace Creek, Death Valley National Monument. (T. H. Watkins)

support of both senators in that state's delegation, the California Desert Protection Act languished in Washington. It continued moribund during 1987—though joined by a companion bill in the House introduced by Congressman Mel Levine—was reintroduced again early in 1988, and—after a short-lived period when it seemed that Wilson might agree to a workable compromise—stalled again. As Congress reconvened early in 1989 with a new presidential administration at the helm, both Cranston and Levine doggedly pushed forward their respective protection bills, while the Bureau of Land Management pressured a reelected Senator Wilson to introduce his own bill, one based largely on its California Desert Plan, and the conservation community geared up for one more chapter in the long struggle to save the desert.

It probably would have saddened the great California naturalist, Raymond Cowles, to learn that there still was a fight to be won. He was gone by then, but he had recognized and had summarized the need poignantly almost twenty years before:

What is left of the unspoiled desert spaces are the last fragments of virgin nature remaining in many parts of the Southwest. They are hospitable to those who accord them their due respect and who have the knowledge to enjoy their intimate little canyons, their wide sun-drenched plains, and the plants and animals that live there. The desert has various aesthetic and scientific satisfactions. It is as deserving of preservation as forests, lakes, and coastlines. Its future merits more than a scourge of off-road vehicles and a population encouraged to growth by irrigation from desalted sea water and other costly sources. Unless we act now we will surely lose these once almost inviolate refuges, which not only serve to harbor wildlife, but which provide valuable sanctuaries of escape from the multiplying pressures of the human world today.

THE PLACE
3. The Long, Secret Mountains

I N *THE COLORADO,* HIS LUMINOUS history of the Colorado River and its country, Frank Waters told the story of a young man he called only Jenkins. In the 1920s, this sturdy individual had been hired by the Bell System to patrol its continental telephone line between Whitewater in the Imperial Valley and Yuma, just across the river in Arizona. He was, in effect, "a lineman for the county," and the road he traveled took him a hundred miles down the valley between the Salton Sea on the southwest and the long, gray wall of the Chocolate Mountains on the northeast. On one such trip, Waters accompanied Jenkins on his rounds and was astonished to learn that when the man climbed telephone poles during the frequent high winds that came down off the mountains, he would turn his face directly into the wind while he worked — this in spite of the killing sand that was driven into his eyes and skin as a result. It was not that the work demanded this of him; in fact, he could have done it better and safer if he had simply turned his back to the wind and the abrading sand. Time after time, Waters watched him repeat this strange and unnecessary ritual before he learned what was behind it. Waters wrote:

Jenkins finally confessed, "It's those mountains," he said with a foolish, frightened smile. Those wrinkled, dried-up desert mountains. He just couldn't turn his back on them. They gave a fellow the creeps. It was like they were looking at you all the time, following you wherever you went. Somehow you just had to keep your eye on them all the time. "But one of these fine days, goddam it!" he said with a peculiar exasperation, "I'm just going to walk off from this here truck and go see what's what!"

In his inarticulate fashion, that young lineman of long ago felt the strange power that is characteristic of all the long mountains that range through the southern third of the California Desert from Interstate 40 to the Mexican border, the Colorado River to the edge of the coastal plain. Geomorphically, they are little different from most of the mountains of the desert, but there is no denying their special feeling. Perhaps it is the quality of light and air here in the southern reaches; the desert haze that is common to the rest of the region is somehow deeper, bluer — more hazy — perhaps because of a higher moisture content that comes from evaporation off the long, man-made lakes on the lower stem of the Colorado, or the Gulf of California to the south, or even that great salty lake called the Salton Sea. In these misty distances the mountains rise like monsters with secrets at their heart. "Great hairless shapes with dry scaly skins," Waters wrote, "they look like immense lizards basking in the sun. . . . Like heavy molten mountains of lead. Like mountains of the moon. No feature of any landscape on earth exerts their fascinating appeal."

Too grim a description, many would say. For there is real beauty, as well as dark imaginings, to be found in all the mountains that blister the land south and west of the East Mojave. Consider, for instance, the Old Woman Mountains, a range that humps its "great hairless shape" above the Ward Valley fifty miles southwest of Needles. There is plenty of mystery to be followed here, if mystery is what you are after — both the Mojave and Chemehuevi Indians invested the mountains

The hidden pools of Carrizo Falls in the In-Ko-Pah Mountains. (Terrence Moore)

This view of the
Stepladder Mountains
shows a wide variety of
vegetation existing in
the desert region.
(Barbara Reber/
California Desert
Protection League)

Looking down into a
springtime valley in the
Turtle Mountains. (Mike
McWherter/California
Desert Protection
League)

with mythic qualities, and ancient campsites and even burial areas can be found. But the huge complex of fault-block mountains also contain sheer rock walls, deep canyons, sandy washes, large interior valleys well-wooded with juniper and piñon pine, rocky spires of splendid dimensions, and at least sixteen springs and the wildlife they nurture, including bighorn sheep, mule deer, and many species of birds.

Looming above the southeastern side of the Ward Valley are the Turtle Mountains, another large expanse (the Old Woman Mountains and the Turtle Mountains are two of the largest proposed wildernesses contained in the California Desert Protection Act). The northeastern end of the mountains is strikingly colorful, being composed mainly of volcanic rocks ranging in hue from red to pink, gold, brown, and tan, which wind and sand and rain have carved into spires and sharp-edged peaks and into which ancient streams and modern flash floods have cut deep, narrow canyons whose banded, slickrock beauty is a match for that of the better-known canyons of southern Utah. Here, too, the Indians have left

their marks, and eleven important springs feed an abundance of desert wildlife and numerous plant species—including, in Chemehuevi Wash, such Sonoran Desert types as ironwood, palo verde, smoke tree, and crucifixion thorn, all of which find their northernmost ranges here. Mopah Spring, a main watering hole for the Turtle Mountains bighorn sheep herd, features a small cluster of fan palms—this, too, the northernmost appearance of the species (though probably transplanted here in the 1920s).

The Old Woman Mountains and the Turtle Mountains do not stand alone in the wide plain of the southcentral desert—the Marble, Clipper, Piute, Stepladder, Chemehuevi, and Whipple mountains all curve their rocky flanks above them, from the Clipper Valley below the southwestern corner of the East Mojave to Parker Dam on the Colorado River. But there is nothing quite so impressive as they between their southwestern slopes and Joshua Tree National Monument—although the Cadiz Dunes in the heart of the Cadiz Valley are unique in that in the shadowed swales beneath their curving pyramids one can

find tiny pockets of water where a surprising bouquet of life springs up—wildflowers often bloom here long after others have pulled in their blossoms elsewhere in the desert.

Like Death Valley in the north and East Mojave in the center, the central fact in the southern third of the California Desert is Joshua Tree National Monument—and it has its own secret mountains, to boot. Virtually every acre of the monument that does not have roads or other civilized improvements was designated official wilderness in 1976; as outlined earlier, conservationists would like to expand the monument, add even more wilderness, and make it a national park. And for good reason, for there is nothing quite like this place anywhere else. This is definitive high desert, with elevations ranging from 1,000 feet in the Pinto Basin at the monument's eastern end to more than 6,000 feet in the Little San Bernardino Mountains along its southwestern edge. It also is a transition zone between Sonoran and Mojave desert types, a place where one can see, for example, patches of ocotillo mixing with patches of cholla. Throughout the long

basin that slowly increases in elevation under the shadow of the Pinto Mountains on its northern edge, the most extensive forests of some of the largest Joshua trees in the California Desert mix with other species of yucca (the Joshua itself is a species of giant yucca, and here it can reach heights of 40 feet), numerous cacti, possibly the most varied and extensive beds of desert wildflowers found anywhere—which blossom in the wettest springs like laughter in a crowded theater—no fewer than five fan-palm oases, and huge boulder gardens, where enormous mounds of blocked and faulted granite stones the size of suburban cottages are piled up like the petrified droppings of some monstrous prehistoric creature.

The fan palm oases of Joshua Tree National Monument are some of its most endearing features; in this waterless land, there is something unexpectedly lush about the sight of the fat, green heads of fan palms bending together over a spring in some hidden notch of the mountains, their long, graceful fronds clicking and rustling gently with every breeze. And the mountains of Joshua

Sunset in the Turtle Mountains. (Terrence Moore)

Tree are not the only ones to harbor these little green islands in the great island of the desert. Down in the Chuckwalla Mountains some forty miles south of the southeastern border of the monument is a place called Corn Springs, which—along with a diverse collection of ocotillo, palo verde trees, and desert ironwood— harbors one of the largest palm oases in the desert. Much smaller but no less entrancing oases can be found cunningly hidden in the mazelike and wonderfully complex sandstone canyons of the Orocopia Mountains and the Mecca Hills just a few miles northeast of the sprawling, irrigated metropolis of Indio in the Coachella Valley. Much farther south, down in the Jacumba Mountains, wedged between the boundary of Anza-Borego Desert State Park and the Mexican border, are a few more—some of which may have slaked the thirst of Spanish colonists in the eighteenth century, for it was through the Yuha Desert just to the east of the mountains that they established one leg of their "land bridge" between Sonora, Mexico, and the California settlements. The oases indisputably supplied both historic and prehistoric Indian peoples, for the region is dotted throughout with ancient cultural artifacts, ranging from petroglyphs to campfire rings.

The shadowed, pastel beauty of the mountains in the southern desert is captured nicely in this view of the Marble Mountains. (Suzi Moore)

Mopah Peak as seen from the palm oasis at Mopah Spring. (Terrence Moore)

Late afternoon in the
Cadiz Dunes between
the Old Woman
Mountains and the
Sheephole Valley. (Suzi
Moore)

A well-bouldered
canyon in Joshua Tree
National Monument.
(Terrence Moore)

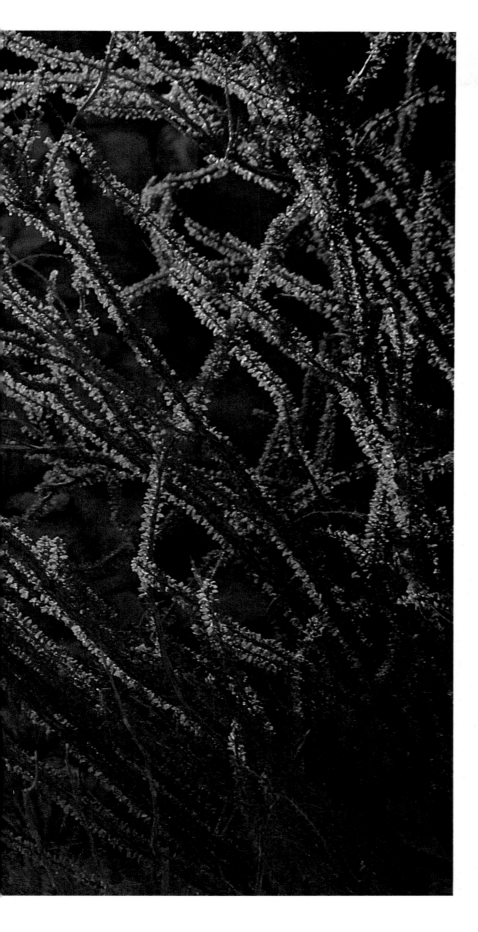

M ORE THAN A HUNDRED MILES EAST OF the sweltering Yuha Desert, past the U.S. Naval Aerial Gunnery Ranges in the West Mesa, through the town that water built—El Centro—and through the fields of melons and winter lettuce and alfalfa patches and cattle feedlots and cotton fields of the Imperial Valley, beyond the Algodones Dunes and Pilot Knob Mesa, roughly paralleling the swinging bend the Colorado River makes as it curls around in a southwesterly direction on its snakey way to Mexico and then the Gulf of California (at least during those years that are wet enough for the river to make it all the way to the Gulf)—in this place are a final set of mountains to consider in this cookless tour of the California Desert.

An ocotillo backlit by
the sun—one of the
plants common to the
Sonoran segment of the
California Desert.
(Terrence Moore)

Desert palms at Corn
Spring in the Little
Chuckwalla Mountains.
(Terrence Moore)

Larkspur in the Santa
Rosa Mountains. (Suzi
Moore)

Sunset in the Little
Picacho Mountains.
(Terrence Moore)

These are the Picacho Mountains, a heavily eroded range that rises from near sea level on the edge of the Colorado to a height of nearly 2,000 feet in Picacho Peak. They are not as spectacular as, say, the Turtle Mountains or the Inyos or even the Old Dad Mountains, but they have their moments—the splintered, ragged peaks that thrust suddenly from rolling, and sometimes almost entirely flat, expanses of land; labyrinthine canyons and washes that hold accumulations of such diverse Sonoran Desert plants as jojoba, bur sage, blue palo verde, smoke trees, and velvet mesquite; volcanic mesas and spectacular views east into Arizona, south into Mexico, and west into California.

And secrets. Human beings have been in these mountains for as many millennia as they have been anywhere in the California Desert—and probably more than most, for the river valley below the mountains is a welcoming place.

They hunted bighorn sheep and mule deer in the mountains, and because the mountains gave them food, the people gave them myths and legends. They crossed the mountains on trading expeditions to the coast through Indian Pass, and buried their dead in the rolling valleys. They made a home here in a place they learned to use, respect, and probably even love, in spite of the demands it made on them for survival. And maybe that is the message of these mountains, of this desert. Frank Waters thought so. He wrote movingly of all who had passed through, settled in, or tried to conquer the California Desert. "On them all," he wrote, "space and solitude set their mark; they are an intangible dimension of our own lives. They remain, not to be conquered but only to be understood. That is their only secret."

Epilogue

THE SUN IS LOWER IN THE SKY AND THE SHADOWS begin to slant significantly as I study out the ground of my returning. It is going to be harder to get down from this high place on the side of a ridge in the New York Mountains than it was getting up to it earlier in the day. I do not want to negotiate again the dangerous cascade of rocks that fills the ravine at my feet. At the same time, I do not want to find myself clinging to the side of a mountain in the dark, either. With my binoculars I search out the flag of a red shirt I had tied to the branch of a piñon pine this morning before setting out. It is on the edge of a sandy little bench at the top of the first ridge I had climbed when I came up from the valley floor, perhaps 1,500 feet below me, perhaps more, where I had left my sleeping bag and big backpack for a dry camp this evening. Finding the shirt waving gently in the breeze, I sweep the glasses back up the ridge to where it joins the rest of the mountain maybe half a mile directly across from me; if I can cut across the slope of the mountain to this point, it looks as if I can follow the ridge line almost straight down to my camp with a minimum of stony scrambles. Worth a try, anyway. I put my half-empty water bottle and my thoroughly empty gorp bag into my day pack, snug my camera to my dandy Cuban hitch, adjust the binoculars around my neck, and set off in a direct line for my target.

I do not get anywhere near it. This country is never what it seems to be. I had forgotten that. Even when it does not indulge in the ultimate distortion of mirage, the country hides its shapes and distances with a wonderful dexterity—mountain peaks are three or four times farther from you than they appear to be, are bigger than they appear to be, are a different *color* than they appear to be. And gullies become ravines become canyons— and, looked at from an angle too close to the ground, disappear altogether into a confused mosaic of stones and scrub. That is what has happened to me here. The difficult but apparently negotiable path I had traced out in my mind's eye has vanished over the edge of the first hidden ravine, not big enough to be called a canyon, but deep enough to be called a major inconvenience. Doggedly, I clamber down one side, testing each stone, clinging to the exposed roots of piñon pine and greasewood, then pull myself up the other.

Piñon pine and rock wall in the New York Mountains.
(T. H. Watkins)

After perhaps forty or fifty yards, I discover another ravine, this one even deeper and steeper, and repeat the gingerly struggle down, the heave-and-haul up. Then another. After working my way up out of the third ravine, I decide that this is not working out. I have come upon a network of ravines like spokes on a wheel; God only knows how many more there are between me and the ridge that is supposed to lead me back to my sleeping bag. The sun is even lower in the sky now. The air has a touch of November chill in it. There is only one thing to do, I decide—go into the next ravine and follow it down into the swiftly shadowing and unseeable terrain below it. If I keep moving toward the east, I tell myself, sooner or later I will make it to the foot of the slope that will lead me up to the sandy bench where my shirt flaps bravely in the wind.

So down I climb—and continue climbing, crawling, and sliding on my butt down the ravine, which is not quite as jammed with stone and brush and cactus as the slit I had climbed this morning—a year ago?—but is every bit as steep. Even worse, when I get to what appears to be its bottom, it is not the bottom; it is a shelf of rock that juts out over a fifty-foot drop to a nest of big, sharp-edged stones. I gaze back up the ravine; from here it looks like the stairway from Hell, and I am not at all certain I have the strength to crawl back up. I turn back to the drop-off, sit down, scoot out to the edge and look down. It is not a completely vertical drop, it seems, and there appear to be a number of cunningly placed ledges in the face of the rock, each of them no more than three or four inches wide and maybe twice that in length, but possibly enough to make a foothold. Besides, I don't really have much of a choice. I take my daypack off and put both camera and binoculars into it, then put it back on, roll onto my stomach and slowly push myself over the edge feet first.

Ever so slowly, every inch of my body from fingertips to toetips clinging to the surface of the rock, I slide down to the first ledge, my eyes closed, my cheek pressed against the stone. I arrive with a jolt, open my eyes, creep along the protuberance in order to get an angle on the next little ledge, then let myself go again. Four times I perform this ritual before I am sitting on the rocks at the bottom, looking up. It is quite a while before I realize that I have been talking to myself; it is only a little while longer before I realize I have been praying.

Nothing else I encounter is quite so immediately dangerous as I slowly work my way down through the tangled maze of rocks and ridges and gullies, though there is no shortage of opportunities for a broken leg or arm or head. The seats of both my jeans *and* my underpants have been mutilated by all the butt-sliding I have been doing; only strings of fabric remain, and I would make a dandy photograph for someone with a crude sense of humor. Time is my principal enemy now. The setting sun has tinted the peaks from which I have descended with a mellow, golden brightness, but down here there is less light every minute, and in perhaps another hour it will be too dark to continue scrambling safely. It would hardly kill me to be forced to scratch out a place to sleep in a sandy corner somewhere in this rocky mess. I have almost a quart of water left, and it would be more than enough to last me until morning light enabled me to see my way out of here. But

I am sore and tired and hungry, and I remember with a certain clarity the softness of the patch of sand in which I had chosen to roll out my bag that morning, the shelter of the big rock in whose lee the sand patch lay, the fat sack of hand-assembled gorp that waits for me, the luxurious prospect of taking off my tattered pants and tucking into the slick warmth of my bag. I continue my staggering progress down the mountain.

At least my sense of direction has not deserted me, for perhaps forty-five minutes later I look up in relief at the shoulder of the bench where the beacon of my shirt can still be seen in the fading light. By the time I have climbed to the top, untied the shirt, and found my bag and big pack, the sun has set with a glorious burst of color and the desert is being colored faintly by the lavender of a short-lived twilight. I get out of my pants and into my sleeping bag and open the bag of gorp, watching the valley below me slowly fill with darkness as I munch upon nuts and berries and yogurt chips.

This kind of solitary excursion is frowned upon in certain circles—those occupied by my father, for instance; he had gently reminded me earlier that one should never hike alone in rough country. This is true enough, and there had been moments up there on the mountain when I had reason to consider the wisdom of his warning. If something had happened to me in one of those dark clefts, the chances of being rescued—or even of being found—would have been slim. I had dismissed that thought from my mind, though.

The question remains as to why I had gone up into those rocks alone. It was not an articulated quest, a deliberate seeking after some kind of mystical connection. I am not that kind of pilgrim. I had seen no visions when I climbed as far as the mountain would let me, nor had the Raven come to croak my secret name. But I cannot deny that there has been some kind of testing going on here—self-imposed, of course, but no less challenging (or stupid, depending upon one's point of view) for that. An old friend with whom I had gone hiking in southern Utah in May of this same year may have cut close to the truth when he wrote about my propensities in a later article (never consort with writers). He has known me long enough to be familiar with my exploits on both sides of a personal watershed and spoke with a certain authority: "It was as if he were trying to make up for lost time, which in fact he was. Having spent the worst part of his years as a fellow of rather limited ambulatory experience, as an armchair, or bar stool, elitist if you will, [he] had recently undergone a change of life and become—transmogrified—a compleat walker, a seeker of solitude, a bagger of boondocks. . . . I have reason to suspect that he harbors a certain predilection for risk."

Well, yes, but I prefer to call it testing—a kind of proving to myself (who else would there be?) that I can still earn the right to be alone here in a hard and beautiful and empty country, no matter what mean failings there have been in my past. I know that I can never reclaim the lost years; they sit in the middle of my life like a black hole. But the sweat, pain, fear, and exhilaration of winning, alone and unassisted, the chance to look out forty miles to the horizon from a rock that may never have been warmed by a human rear end before is one way I have of measuring the strength of my survival.

It has been this desert, this island trapped in time, surrounded on all sides by everything that would destroy its silence and its beauty, that has given me the opportunity to taste the wine of solitude and prove up on my life once again. There are other landscapes that offer the solace of open spaces, to borrow from Gretel Ehrlich, and I have been in many of them. But there is something in this hard-edged land, in the arid simplicity of its elements, that speaks to me with more power than others I have known, and I do not think it is just the resonance of memory. John Steinbeck felt it, driving through this country in 1962:

> *"At night in this waterless air, the stars come down just out of reach of your fingers. In such a place lived the hermits of the early church piercing to infinity with unlittered minds. . . . And there are true secrets in the desert. In the war of sun and dryness against living things, life has its secrets of survival.*

Just so. I wonder, as I put away my gorp bag and water bottle and slide down into the silky welcome of my sleeping bag, I wonder how much longer the spectacular civilization that encircles this island can afford to pretend that it does not really need to learn those secrets any more, that the quantums of technology will be quite sufficient to provide for the future as one century tilts into another. How long will it be, I wonder, before our civilization realizes that the desert wilderness is not—as our history has always insisted—a threat that must be overcome, but a protection to be embraced? That if this fine, wild place so close to where it is most deeply needed is lost to blind expedience, one of the last rings of safety that preserve us from ourselves will be gone. Where then escape?

The sky above me has turned to ink. There are no answers and there is no moon. Only the stars; the stars; the stars.